Anna Maria's Needleworks Notebook

ANNA MARIA HORNER

WILEY

John Wiley & Sons, Inc.

Credits

SENIOR EDITOR
Roxane Cerda

SENIOR PROJECT EDITOR
Donna Wright

COPY EDITOR
Marylouise Wiack

EDITORIAL MANAGER
Christina Stambaugh

VICE PRESIDENT AND PUBLISHER
Cindy Kitchel

**VICE PRESIDENT AND
EXECUTIVE PUBLISHER**
Kathy Nebenhaus

INTERIOR DESIGN
Tai Blanche

COVER DESIGN
Susan Olinsky

PHOTOGRAPHY
Anna Maria Horner

Anna Maria's
Needleworks
Notebook

✕ ✕ ✕ ✕ ✕

This book is dedicated to my talented grandmothers,
Anna Ruth Coble and Eleni Demacopoulos, who both lived
long enough to see their gifts manifested in my efforts.
Their voices live within me each time I pick up needle
and thread. Their spirits are present in the motion blur
of my hand working every day. I pray to leave even a
fraction of that inspiration to my own family.

✕ ✕ ✕ ✕ ✕

Acknowledgments

As with any project that ends up in the hands of many, it took a lot of people to make this book possible. My editors, Roxane Cerda and Donna Wright, have been so patient and gracious in both their willingness and support in letting me try a different way of making a book. They, together with my publisher, Cindy Kitchel, have worked so hard to ensure my vision for this project rests at the center of every small goal along the way. I owe a great deal to their trust in me and their friendship.

Pierrette Abegg, my assistant, has been a sweet, solidifying source in this project as well as countless others. I am thankful for her willingness to help with every major and minor task, even if I doubled them out of indecisiveness. Her effervescent father, Jimmy Abegg, is responsible for the cover photos and many good laughs. His lovely photography is both accomplished and appreciated.

Photographing the gorgeous faces of my friends and family in this book allowed me to share the beauty and love that I get to experience every day of my life with a lucky bunch of readers. It has been an honor to include you all on these pages. Thanked in order of appearance are: Eleni Horner, Isabela Horner, Roman Horner, Kelly Gunter, Naomi Daniel, Anna Johnson, Sierra Ragazzo, Juliana Horner, and Lily Katsaitis. I also appreciate the assistance of Pierrette Abegg and Anna Johnson for several photographs.

Thank you to my husband, Jeff, and my children, Juliana, Nicoloas, Joseph, Isabela, Eleni, and Roman. All of you are a source of inspiration, confidence, and joy for me, whether I am stitching, writing, drawing, or dreaming. Thank you for giving me time and encouragement to seek out my own creative happiness. I love you.

And finally to my mom and dad, Mary Lynn and Eleftherios Demacopoulos: Thank you for making sure that all of the beauty that has surrounded you in your lives would also surround me. I love you both dearly.

{ Contents }

Grid Works

Free Works

The Story of My Stitches

My parents would have made the perfect Peace Corps couple. I remember hearing this phrase in my house long before I learned of the actual existence or purpose of the Peace Corps. Both were raised in a farming community—my father in the midst of vineyards in southern Greece, and my mother, the daughter of a veterinarian in a tiny town in northern Indiana. Through many disciplines like crochet, knitting, loomed brocade, embroidery, cross stitch, and needlepoint, each of my grandmothers—on opposite sides of the world—added layers of beauty to their homes with handworked items. So in addition to witnessing and taking part in the daily hard work of maintaining their family's livelihood, my parents were also surrounded by everyday works of refined beauty. While I'm sure they never consciously realized it, it was their absorption of this beauty and their eventual translation of it in their own family that would have everything to do with my own interests and

livelihood. My father became a civil engineer by trade, and my mother a nurse. In the midst of raising my brother, sister, and me, they also endeavored to design, build, paint, repair, sew, mend, hem, stitch, and knit as much of our house together as time and finances would allow.

Though they worked with their own hands (and still do) to create or fortify their home with items that served some necessity, I was most drawn to those works that weren't necessary at all. Surely our walls would have stood even if my father hadn't made beautiful paintings to hang on them. Yet I could describe to you in minute detail how his bold and colorful strokes of oil paint rendered the disturbed water beside a gondola with a long ore at the center of that swirl in a scene framed in our living room. Surely my baby bed sheet and pillowcase would have been just as warm without the elaboration of Dumbo and the whole circus cross stitched across each of them. Yet I have explicit memories of how those bumpy stitches felt under my fingertips and of rubbing them across my lips to drift into sleep. That blanket lived alongside me until I had rubbed out every single stitch except Dumbo's eyes. The surviving pillowcase still rests folded in our linen closet. My sister and I could have busied ourselves with reading or coloring during the everyday napping hour when visiting our family in Greece over the summer. Instead my mother busied us with the regular and meditative craft of needlepoint, which we got to select ourselves from the local "kentima" shop. I can still see that tiny shop packed from floor to ceiling with layers and layers of painted and printed canvases to choose from. Heaven.

Though many of us have come to rely on several elaborate tools for sewing, if we encountered sewing as very young children, before it seemed safe to sew with a machine, we were likely presented with simple tools. Needle. Thread. Cloth. My earliest attempts at hand sewing had everything to do with making something

My baby bedding stitched by my mother.

that was functional. Once threading a needle didn't make my heart race or my fingertips sweat in frustration, I can remember feeling elated at what I could manage. I sewed together doll clothes, quilts for my Barbie, and little patches on this or that. But eventually it was the beauty of the actual stitch and all the possible shapes that stitch could take that would capture my imagination. I began to notice everything around me, and how it was made. It was based on a design, a drawing. Every table in our house had some sort of embellished cloth that protected it from any vase, dish, or object that occupied it regularly. These were usually gifts from my aunts or grandmother in Greece. They weren't always elaborate, but each one was well designed and diligently worked. What still holds me breathless to this day in regards to needlework is how the simplest of tools can create the grandest of works and the single, variable element igniting that beauty is the human hand.

You might have guessed (just three paragraphs into this book) that my passion for handwork, and all of my art, comes from a very personal place. This book is therefore an intimate offering of some of my favorite projects with information about the materials I used to create them and the steps I took to complete them. It is a personal journey with various forms of needlework. I use the word *journey*, not because I've charted my beginnings with needlework up until now, but because the process of putting together all of the inspirations, designs, drawings, and notes felt like a journal or a notebook. I wanted to stay true to that diary of sorts in the book's final form in the hopes that you'll feel free to make discoveries with me along the way. Perhaps you'll even begin a companion notebook with mine, where you'll take notes on your progress, create scribbles and sketches on your musings, or whatever you might like to try next.

My father's painting (above) and my own first attempt at needlepoint at 11 years old.

1976
My Yiayia Eleni (left) and mother (right) show the knit blanket they made together. My brother, sister and I (next to my mother) were asked to pose, too.

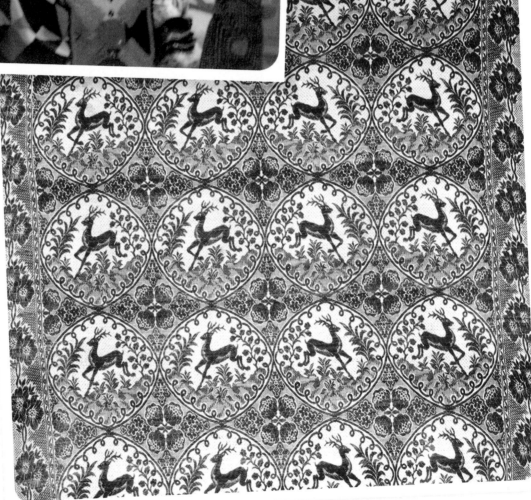

My Yiayia Eleni's handloomed blanket was made with wool, from her own sheep, which she spun and dyed, 1976.

Learning about yourself as a designer and what it is that you can uniquely offer the world through your art is such an epiphany (which can often take years). If I have learned anything, it is that I am an idea girl. I simply have yet to run out of things that I want to try or variations that I'd like to explore based on whatever I just finished yesterday. Specifically with handwork, I cannot stop jotting down various combinations of materials that I would like to try together, a color combination yet to be explored, or the way I might hand-quilt my next patchwork. There are many beautiful books and pattern resources out there for cross stitch, needlepoint, embroidery, and crewel work. The history of these handcrafts throughout the world across dozens of cultures independently and collectively is awe inspiring. Taking the time to research each of them over the years has left me genuinely enriched and entirely motivated to continue *making*. However, my primary goal here is to encourage you with just a little know-how and a lot of inspiration. It is, after all, only a few stitch styles in any discipline that can set you off on a lifetime of work.

I've set out to share these projects in a way that won't leave you wondering what to do with this or that gorgeous piece of handwork once finished; rather, you will have a myriad of options about how to work them into your home, your wardrobe, your gift giving, and your art collection. I wrote about these projects in a similar way to how they are made—with general guides but also with an inspiration to further elaborate. I hope that I've presented these artworks with the same genuine excitement with which they arrived in my mind, losing nothing in the process. I also hope that you, like me, will come to love and not be intimidated by the freedom that needlework offers.

My own ideas don't always land themselves very firmly into one discipline or another; they often combine handwork, sewing, and patchwork all in one project. I don't always *follow the rules*, so to speak, or use the most common materials for a given project. It's important to remember that, really, there are no rules to needlework, or any craft for that matter. There are simply traditions of how any given task or art form is commonly done. These traditions do, however, come about because their processes stand the test of time for either durability or beauty's sake. It is for this reason that I don't believe in completely ignoring them. I like to use tradition in a way that informs me but doesn't restrict me. Needlework traditions are so beautiful and give us such a wonderful foundation from which to learn the basics. Your individual continuation of those skills and what you choose to do with them is something that belongs entirely to you. Your skills will improve and render more beauty one stitch after another. So take up a needle. Just imagine what you will make. It promises to be more than the work of your hands. Perhaps it will also become the work of your heart. Enjoy!

XO
Anna Maria

A family self-portrait printed and stitched while I was in college, 1993.

How to Use this Book

My "notebook" is divided into two main categories of needlework, which in turn cover several disciplines within the general field of embroidery. The Grid Works section is devoted to cross stitch and needlepoint (which some might refer to as tapestry or canvas work). Their use of a grid or graph that you follow in order to stitch gives these two disciplines a great deal in common. Though cross stitch and needlepoint traditionally use materials made of a different fiber content, they are both worked onto a material with a very regular weave or evenweave that dictates the size and scale of every stitch.

The Free Works section is devoted to embroidery and crewel work. I refer to them as *free works* because they are traditionally sewn onto a solid cloth surface that does not dictate the stitch's size or shape. Rather, it is the line work of the actual pattern and the various chosen styles of stitching that determine how the work is made. While this book offers plenty of common stitch styles in the Free Works section, there are enough stitch styles across all embroidery disciplines to fill an encyclopedia.

Both the Grid Works and the Free Works sections are filled with projects that have corresponding patterns to follow in the back of the book unless otherwise noted. Most of the cross-stitch and needlepoint patterns follow a color-coded graph, and the embroidery and crewel work patterns are followed by first tracing some form of provided line work onto cloth. After reading through the overviews and various stitch tutorials in each of the chapters, the notes provided with each project offer further tips for you to complete the project using the patterns at the back of the book. Though all of the pattern pages are perforated for easier use in tracing and keeping your projects mobile, it is up to you whether you tear them out. If you'd like to keep your book fully intact, just transfer the line work of embroidery and crewel patterns to tracing paper first before transferring them to cloth. And rather than tearing out grid patterns to follow, just keep the book alongside you as you work on needlepoint and cross stitch.

Each discipline chapter (cross stitch, needlepoint, embroidery, and crewel work) will offer advice on common tools used and how to develop your own patterns through various techniques and inspirations. Each chapter will also have a section of stitch tutorials that you can refer back to as you complete the projects as well as for future project inspiration. Each project will list the exact materials used in the photographed example right down to the color/number of every thread included.

It is no secret handwork involves a slower process than some other crafts or machine-sewn projects. However, I decided very early in life that the reward was well deserved and more than worth the effort. Needlework does not need to be a process that requires weeks or months (or years). There are projects in this book that can be finished in a matter of a few hours. However, works that are obviously more involved should not be dismissed altogether due to time constraints. Perhaps you would like to try just a single flower in a bouquet design, and not the whole bouquet. When was the last time you were able to finish just a small portion of a machine-sewn blouse and have it work out for you? Exactly. This is the freedom involved with needlework.

The modern sewing industry has done a marvelous job of making sure we know that a pillow can be made in an hour or a skirt in 2 hours with just the right steps and tools. That is a wonderful accomplishment and it has inspired many who might not otherwise be sewing to flock to the latest projects and ideas with enthusiasm. What would be regretful is if the process of making something with your hands simply becomes a race against the clock. In my own work, I feel myself racing against the clock, almost daily. I love my sewing machine work and designing and creating clothing and quilts. I love seeing something finished. Yet as a balance to the swiftness of a lot of quick tricks, and plowing through mountains of fabric in a month's time, I am grateful for the time that it does take to complete works by hand. I further feel no shame for the drawerful of my patient, mid-progress needleworks.

With regard to difficulty, I should start by saying that I do not like the phrase "level of difficulty." That even makes me want to give up before I start! Let's call it a level of experience, shall we? I daresay that the projects I've designed here offer something for all experience levels and ages. I honestly believe that there is not a difficult stitch in this book, but rather it might be the combination of many stitches together that can seem overwhelming. Once you have dissected them you might find yourself surprised at how doable the designs really are. You can only make one stitch at a time anyway, so why worry about all the neighboring ones until you get to them? With cross stitch and needlepoint, the stitches are extremely simple, so it's a great place to start and an especially great craft for kids to pick up because of the regularity of the stitches. Many of the embroidery and crewel work vignettes are just a handful of simple stitches but it's their direction, color, and concentration that give the designs depth and interest. Getting back to that notion of freedom, there is nothing wrong with taking a design like the Loves Me Bouquet (page 99) and using the pattern to create a work more like those in the Coloring Book Collection (page 86). The elaboration level of any work is completely up to you so turn it into something that you will relish!

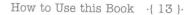

Grid Works

The projects in this section are devoted to two very beautiful needlework traditions, cross stitch and needlepoint. I've included them together because in their most basic form, each craft is designed and executed on a grid or graph, using a very regular stitch style. These are often called *counted works* because the pattern work for both disciplines is a chart made up of tiny blocks of color or symbols that denote certain colors that you count up, down, left, and right to keep your place as you stitch. Both cross-stitch and needlepoint patterns are available already printed onto the cloth or canvas to avoid having to count at all, so that you can stitch by color as you go. While using a preprinted or hand-painted canvas design for needlepoint is the most common way to take part in that craft, using a coded chart for counting and stitching is the most common cross-stitch pattern format.

Just as their patterns follow a grid, so does the structure of the cloth onto which each craft is worked. Cloth that is suitable for cross stitch has been woven in a way that the *warp* (vertical) threads and the *weft* (horizontal) threads are spaced evenly from one another and the intersections of the warp and weft happen at perfectly regular intervals so that the resulting grid of woven fabric is completely square. This cloth, usually cotton or linen, is called *evenweave*. The most typical cloth for needlepoint is a canvas, which is a much sturdier surface, with a more open and obvious grid of threads for working the needlepoint stitches. While the materials are very different, they are both defined in terms of thread count per inch of cloth. So if there are 11 warp threads across an inch of needlepoint canvas, your needlepoint will have 11 stitches per inch because you work a single stitch around every warp/weft intersection. With evenweave cloth for cross stitch, however, the threads are very tightly packed. Many of the cross-stitch projects in the following chapter are worked onto 28-count evenweave. But because you work a single cross stitch onto the intersection of *two* warp threads and *two* weft threads, your finished work will have just 14 stitches per inch.

More fabric notes will be covered in greater detail before you begin the projects, but for now it's most important to remember that any design set onto a graph can be worked for either cross stitch or needlepoint. As is the case here, you've probably purchased designs for completing specific patterns, but coming up with your own design might be simpler than you think and can actually be quite fun. For the modern, computer-literate needleworker, it might make more sense to think of cross stitch and needlepoint patterns simply as pixelated art. In other words, it's a form or design that has been broken down into individual blocks of color. When you think of patterns that way, you'll realize that with something as simple as graph paper or as high-tech as your computer you can create a myriad of designs for either or both types of needlework.

Traditional cross stitch is most often worked with some air between the stitched elements. In other words, the finished piece allows you to see the background cloth on which the design is stitched. Not only does this mean that you should choose the color of your evenweave cloth carefully, but it also means that the design elements are often more sparse and open and perhaps more simple to design. Conversely, needlepoint is most often worked so that the canvas is not showing at all once the work is complete. Every single intersection of woven canvas has been filled with a stitch. So this tells you that when creating a design for needlepoint you need to consider how the entire space will be filled with stitches all the way to each edge of the canvas.

Design with Graph Paper

When designing your own patterns on graph paper, be sure to keep scale and thread count in mind. Each box of graph paper that you color in will represent a single stitch on the worked surface. What might appear as a large design on your graph paper could end up to be a pretty small design once stitched onto a high thread–count material. So it might be helpful to first determine how many inches tall you want your design to be and then mark those dimensions off on your graph paper. To do this, divide the squares on the graph paper into 1-inch sections based on your stitch count. For example, if the material you are working will have 14 stitches per inch, draw a new grid on top of your graph paper lines to help your planning. Do this by drawing squares that each represent an inch, which in this example is 14 squares tall and 14 squares wide. If the design you want is larger than one sheet of graph paper, simply tape a few pages together with clear tape and keep your grids in line.

Keeping all of this in mind, the following is a collection of ideas and tips for turning various images into patterns for cross stitch or needlepoint using graph paper.

An Alphabet

Though this book provides a lowercase alphabet collection (AlphaCute, page 40), maybe you have a favorite font that you would prefer to use, or maybe you would like to make a larger-scale uppercase monogram. Simply printing out the letters (at a size that accounts for the scale difference between the graph paper and your evenweave) and tracing them onto graph paper would help you create your own alphabet. If you can't see through your graph paper well enough, and you don't own a light table, just treat your computer screen as a light table. You can temporarily tape the graph paper onto the screen. Once the letters are scaled to the size you want on the screen, lightly trace the outline of the letter onto the graph paper. After taking the design down, fill in all the squares that cover the letter's shape very lightly with pencil. When you've had a chance to look at the shape and perfect it, you can color over the lightly shaded squares with colored pencil using a palette that corresponds with your thread palette and possibly adding some design details.

Favorite Fabric

Perhaps you have some cherished fabrics in your stash that have florals or other elements that you would like to see stitched onto cloth. Secure the freshly pressed piece of fabric onto a flat surface with tape. Lay a sheet of tracing paper over the fabric and tape it in place. Draw around the shapes, tracing out various color sections using a pencil first, and then once your lines are perfected, remove the fabric from underneath and trace over the pencil lines in black ink. Because of the scale difference between your graph paper and stitch count (mentioned previously), you might want to enlarge your ink drawing at a copy store to get it to a scale where tracing onto the graph paper will give you the size you want. As suggested with the alphabet, after tracing the outlines lightly onto the graph paper, you can fill in the various color sections with colored pencil and with the luxury of using the original fabric piece as your guide for color.

Your Art

If you fancy yourself an expert doodler, there is no reason why you can't begin your cross stitch or needlepoint with your own imagination. Perhaps you can base a work on one of your own existing paintings or drawings. Use the tips mentioned previously to transfer them to graph paper and color accordingly. Even making the simplest geometric designs on graph paper can create gorgeous results. As exemplified in Border Beauties (shown on page 34), one simple motif repeated over and over again can be stunning. Kids almost always love using graph paper, too (I should know because I can never find mine). So letting them design their own motifs and then stitching them out

with a little help from you can be incredibly rewarding for you both.

If you are even a little computer savvy, you might be more interested in creating digital designs for cross stitch and needlepoint on your computer. There are several reasonably priced charting applications and software applications out there that are pretty simple to learn. Once you get the hang of how to use them, they definitely save time compared to coloring in a bunch of little squares by hand, especially if you are creating a large-scale work where you might want the freedom to digitally edit and not have to erase pencil. These applications allow you to create designs from scratch, or you can import any existing artwork or photograph on your desktop. It will transform the art into a charted graph based on your input of how large you'd like it to be, what stitch count you'd like it to have, and how many colors you'd like the final design to have. It will even tell you by brand which shades of floss or wool to purchase for completing the work. Pretty fancy.

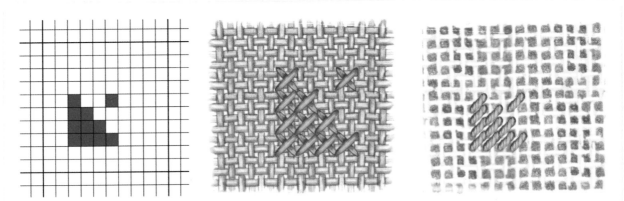

The above shows an example of how a single graphed design element would translate to either cross stitch or needlepoint.

Design with Gimp

I design most of my grid works on the computer using the same art editing program that I use for all of my textile design and other design work. The program is called Gimp, and it's open source software that you can download from the Internet for free at www.gimp.org. It works on several operating systems including Windows, Mac, and my personal favorite, Linux. The program is similar to Adobe Photoshop or Illustrator. While it doesn't have any specific needlework charting tricks like commercial software does, it offers a few features that can help you create a graph to build a design digitally. There are also features that will "pixelize" existing artwork, over which you can lay a digital graph so that you are left with a full-color chart to follow as you stitch. I've detailed the steps to do both in the following section.

NOTE: Keep in mind that all of the settings I have specified in the following instructions scale the graph and/or artwork to show roughly 14 stitches (squares) per inch. (This scale is not to be confused with the thicker lines that simply denote 10 x 10 squares to help you keep your place as you stitch.) You might, however, choose cloth or canvas with a stitch count other than 14. You can still follow the same graph to create a work that has more or fewer stitches per inch. To find out how many inches the design will be, count the total number of squares in the height and width, and then divide each number by your desired stitch count (your cloth will determine this). For example, if your design is 75 squares in height and 120 squares in width, and you will be using a 14-stitch size, the final work will be 5.36" high x 8.57" wide. If you want a different size, simply readjust the settings for both the digital graph and the Pixelize filter until it's the size you want.

Create a Digital Graph

The following is a list of steps for using Gimp to create a simple graph for coloring in a design:

1 Under the FILE tab, select New and create an image size in inches with a resolution of 300 dpi (dots per inch).

2 Under the FILTER tab, select Render > Pattern > Grid.

3 In the Grid dialog box:

- Set the Width at 1 pixel and Height at 1 pixel, leaving the intersection at 0

- Set the Spacing at .07 and .07 inches, leaving the intersection at .07

- Set the Offset at 0 and 0 pixels, leaving the intersection at 0

- Click the color tabs, and select black in each of them

- Click OK

These settings give you a graph that is roughly 14 squares per inch.

Your grid now appears in black line form on the white background.

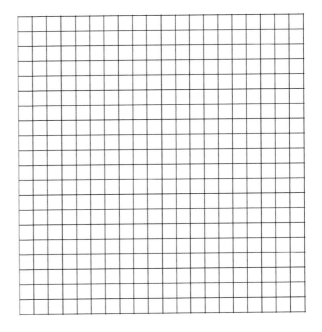

Using thicker lines makes following a pattern much easier, which is why the grid patterns in this book include them. To create additional thicker lines every 10 x 10 squares, follow these steps:

4 Repeat Steps 1–3, except make the following setting changes in the Grid dialog box in Step 3:

- Set the Width at 3 pixels and the Height at 3 pixels, leaving the intersection at 0
- Set the Spacing at .7 and .7 inches, leaving the intersection at .7
- Set the Offset at 0 and 0 pixels, leaving the intersection at 0
- Click the color tabs, and select black in each of them
- Click OK

Draw Your Design

To begin filling in the squares and creating your design, follow these steps:

1 Select the Bucket Fill tool from the Toolbox window. Make sure that the Affected Area is set to "Fill similar colors."

2 Select colors by clicking the foreground color square in the Toolbox.

3 To begin your design, hover the Bucket Fill tool over a square on the graph, and click to fill it.

4 Continue to switch out colors as desired, and simply set Bucket Fill to white when you want to erase.

5 Save the design as a JPEG to your desktop, and print it out when you're ready to begin stitching.

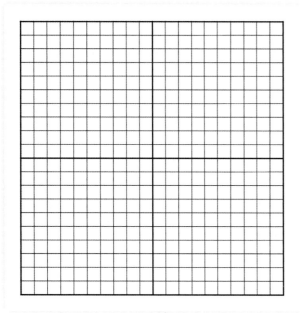

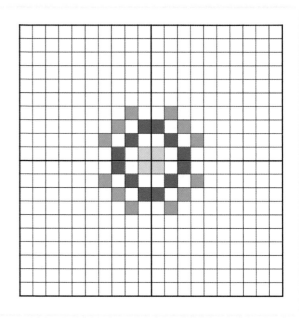

Graph Existing Artwork

To create a grid over an existing digital artwork, just open the existing artwork in Gimp. I recommend first creating a duplicate image so that you have a saved copy of the original artwork.

1   Open your image under the FILE tab.

2   Under the IMAGE tab, select Duplicate. This gives you a new Untitled image.

Make sure the scale of the artwork is set to your desired size in inches at 300 dpi. You can follow Steps 1–4 in "Create a Digital Graph." This lays a black grid (with thin and thick lines) over your artwork, which you can use to stitch the design. Because your design might have irregular organic forms, several squares on the graph will likely have more than one color in them. I recommend reducing those boxes to one color, which typically is whichever color would occupy most of the space within that box. (You can choose the color you want by clicking the Color Picker tool over the desired color in the artwork—the tool icon looks like an eyedropper.) By editing the graph in this way, you'll make the chart that much easier to follow. You can then follow Steps 1–4 in "Draw Your Design" to begin recoloring the design to simplify the grid.

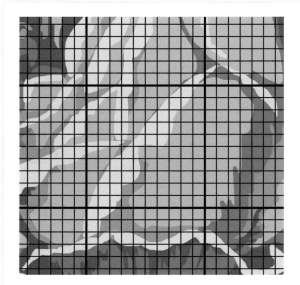 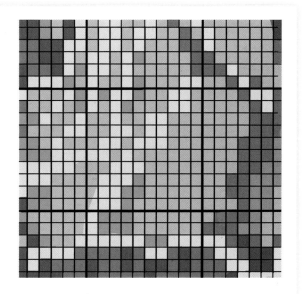

Pixelize Your Artwork

The most enhanced feature that Gimp offers for creating a charted design is a filter called Pixelize. Like the filters in commercial software packages, this filter changes your artwork into a pixelated image. I would first create a duplicate image of your artwork and scale it to your desired size in inches at 300 dpi. Then perform the following steps to pixelize the artwork:

1 Under the FILTER tab, select Blur > Pixelize.

2 In the Pixelize dialog box:
   - In the drop-down menu, select the size format to be inches
   - Set both the Width and Height both to .07
   - Click OK

This will rework your art into a charted artwork. To further clarify one stitch square from another, it's a good idea to lay a black grid over this pixelized art. Just follow the steps in "Create a Digital Graph." As long as you use the same Height and Width settings as you did in the Pixelize filter, the graph will fall right in line with the squares formed by the art. Something to be aware of is that the Pixelize filter will create new colors in the artwork. For example, if the original art contains only 12 colors, the pixelized version may have twice as many, because it is finding shade variations between colors and rendering them for a blurred effect. You'll also notice this around the edges of the artwork where areas that were sharp before the Pixelize filter was applied now create a gradient effect between the image color and the background. As previously mentioned, you can use the Dropper and Bucket Fill tools to perfect the pixelized image as well as to reduce the number of colors to be used in your needlework.

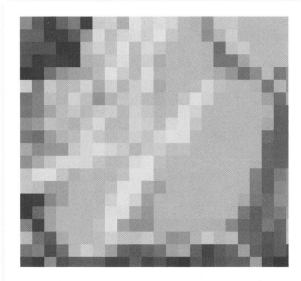

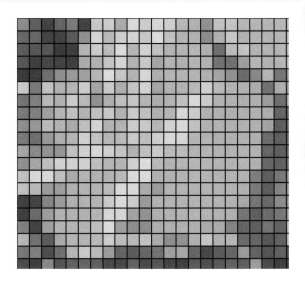

Get to the Good Part

While I love my Gimp software, you might already have a copy of Adobe Photoshop, Adobe Illustrator, or some other art- or photo-editing software with which you're already familiar. So dig around a bit with your digital tools to see if there are similar features that can help you to create a graph or pixelize your artwork. I often find that I can most easily locate a feature in software by performing a quick Internet search. And along those lines, there are lots of free graph paper building tools online to create your own specifically scaled graph paper that you can print or import into your art software.

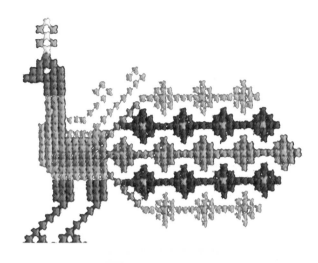

If you try out these techniques, you might just fall in love with them! The process can become quite addictive and before you know it, you'll start wanting to view everything in a pixelized version. Don't forget that photographs are just as easily rendered using these digital methods as artwork is, so just imagine the amazing pattern work that you could develop. Once you've created a pattern to follow, the next challenge is to create a palette of floss or yarns (for cross stitch and needlepoint, respectively) that best matches the colors you've created in your design. There might be a bit of back and forth between altering the colors in your design based on the colors available to you for stitching. It's always best to look at the floss or yarn in person if possible. Once you get the palette right, it's time to make some tea, grab your cloth (or canvas), find a comfortable spot, and get to work.

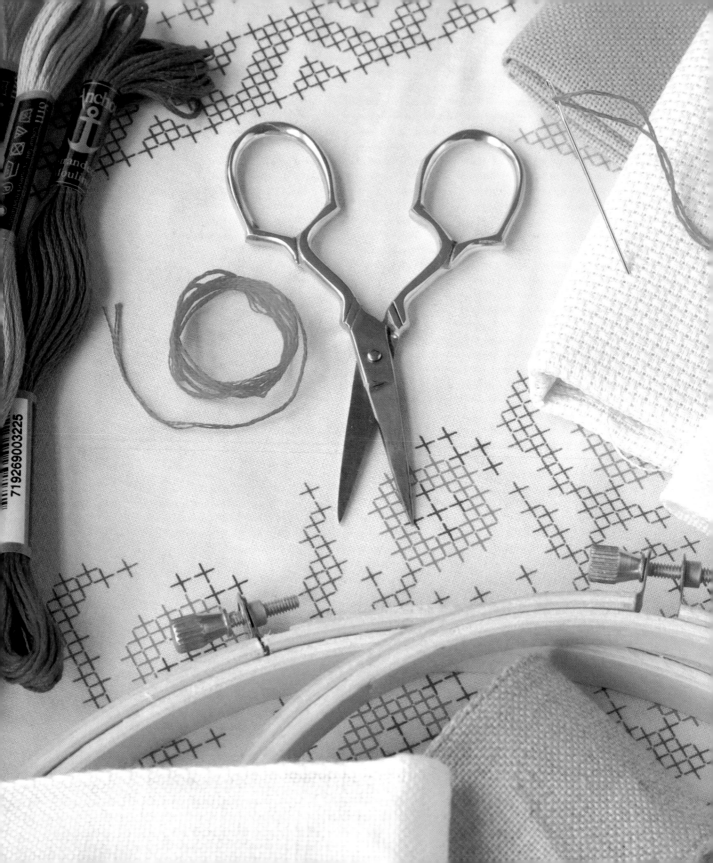

Cross Stitch

Though we covered a bit about the nature of the materials for cross stitch in the introduction to Grid Works, it's time to look a little closer at the cloth that I've used in my own projects and then get to know the little stitch itself. It is so simple—you're going to love it.

Common Materials and Tools

It's been established that to form a perfectly regular and even stitch of any sort, one needs a regular and perfectly even woven cloth (or *evenweave*). Evenweave is most commonly found to be made of either cotton or linen. The fabric is described in count, or the number of threads per inch. A 28-count evenweave has 28 warp (vertical) threads and 28 weft (horizontal) threads intersecting each other in every square inch of material. Thread count sizes can vary from 11 count all the way up to 40 count, which is very fine.

There are several color varieties to choose from, although natural, cream, and pale tones are among the most popular. I found the visual drama of working a design onto black in my Menagerie at Midnight project (see page 28) very exciting, so don't limit yourself. There are also many subcategories of evenweave fabrics that have different textures or patterns running through them, some of which aid in performing certain types of grid work more easily. *Aida cloth* is one such cloth, and it is a perfect material for beginning to cross stitch. The weave is created in a way that exaggerates the look of the square throughout the material so that the holes at each of the four corners of the square are quite obvious and therefore easy to see and stitch through. The count of Aida cloth corresponds directly to your stitch count. Another helpful feature with most Aida cloth is the natural stiff texture it possesses so that in some cases you can forego using any sort of embroidery hoop.

In addition to performing cross stitch on materials specifically designed for it, a product called *waste cloth* can help you turn any fabric—whether bought by the yard for sewing or purchased as a garment—into a surface ready for cross stitch. I use waste cloth in the Crossing the Line projects on page 46. So don't forget as you select which cross-stitch project you'd like to try first, you can actually stitch the pattern on any fabric at all with the help of waste cloth.

On the subject of hoops for cross stitch, if you choose to use one, just experiment and use whatever is most comfortable for you. I tend to switch between several different types, and sometimes I use none at all. I appreciate how lightweight a simple, inexpensive wooden hoop is, but I also like how firmly a heavier plastic hoop holds the material. Each project specifies what I found to work best as I stitched. Overall, I don't worry too much if my worked surface gets tightened into the hoop. I always take the fabric out of the hoop when I'm not working, so this minimizes any disruption to the surface of the stitching.

Unless otherwise specified, all of my cross-stitch projects use Anchor six-strand embroidery floss with varying numbers of strands, which will be specified with each project. I find their threads to be beautifully luminous and of very good quality. (I also work with Anchor to develop product so I, of course, have a biased opinion.) If you use DMC or another brand, there are several online resources that will translate my Anchor color/number notes to the brand you'd like to use. The number of strands that I use depends on the size of the stitches. For smaller stitches I use fewer strands, and larger stitches require more strands. I experimented with this a little bit in the projects, and you might like to as well. I used a basic embroidery needle and embroidery snips for all of my cross-stitch projects in this book.

Stitch Know-how

The actual cross stitch is nothing more than an angled stitch tilted in one direction crossed over a second angled stitch tilted in the opposite direction to form an X. So a single cross stitch is made up of the overlap of two individual stitches. The most desirable surface for cross stitch is one where all the single stitches that pass under to begin the X are tilted in one direction, and all the stitches that pass over to complete the X are tilted in the other direction. Notice in the illustration below that the top thread of the X is always tilted from the top right to the bottom left, overlapping the bottom thread of the X that is always tilted from the top left to the bottom right. The main reason this is desirable is that the light catching the surface of the top thread in each X will illuminate the design in a more uniform fashion if the stitches are tilting in a consistent direction. This is simply an ideal, but please do not fret if you've missed it here and there—I

certainly have. A technique I use, which helps me avoid switching that order, is to always keep the work in my hands with the same up-and-down orientation.

The size of the stitch you make is really up to you, but certain fabrics will dictate a traditional size. With Aida cloth, as explained previously, each X will cover over each of the obvious squares in the material. Of course, that doesn't mean that you couldn't choose to have one X cover over four squares for an exaggerated-size X. This would double the size of any pattern you are following, and you would likely want to increase the number of floss strands you use as well. When using a finer evenweave, I make all of my X's cover over two warp threads and two weft threads. You can see the difference between these two cloths and how they are each stitched in photo (a) (on the next page). So keep in mind with evenweave that if you cover two warp and two weft threads as you stitch, the stitch count per inch will always be half what the thread count of the material is: 28 count will yield 14 stitches per inch, 32 count will yield 16 stitches per inch, and so on.

A good rule to follow when cutting your floss for use is that the length shouldn't be much longer than the distance between your elbow and your fingertips. Rather than knotting the end first, when beginning a cross stitch you work the thread from the back to the front and

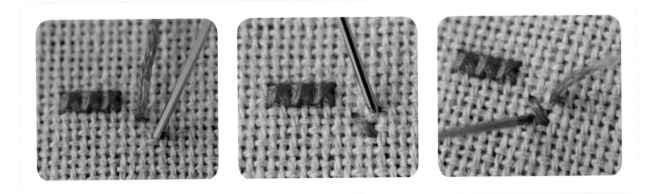

leave a tail of an inch or two. To anchor the tail in place, just make sure that your first few stitches are passing over the tail; you may want to hold the tail underneath in a certain direction to ensure this is happening. When you've come to the end of a thread, simply pass your needle underneath five or six stitches in the back (wrong side) of the work and trim close to the work (b). Beginning the next thread is as simple as passing your needle underneath a group of nearby stitches on the wrong side, then backstitching through one more stitch before surfacing to the right side for stitching.

Following a chart design simply involves making an X with a matching color to the squares of color (or color symbols) that you see on a grid. But making sure you begin in the right place in the cloth requires a small amount of planning. Be sure that your cloth is several inches larger in both directions than the final inch dimensions of your finished pattern design. Find the center point on the chart by counting out squares in both directions, and make a dot. Find the center point of your cloth by folding it in half vertically and then in half horizontally. The point where the two folds meet will be the approximate center of the cloth; you can use a straight pin, or a water soluble pen, to mark that spot.

Begin your design in the center of the work and continue to gradually build out in each direction, keeping your place in the chart by counting over and down, over and up, and so on. It is easier to work nearby whatever section you've just completed than it is to, for instance, finish all of one color throughout the design. The farther you stray from where you've just left off, the easier it is to lose your place or miscount your position. As mentioned in the Create a Digital Graph section on page 19, having a chart that includes thicker lines at every 10 x 10 intersection of squares is helpful in keeping your work in line. All of the chart patterns in this book include those thicker lines. I promise that with just a little practice this will get easier, and you'll be able to more quickly read the shapes on the chart, without too much counting.

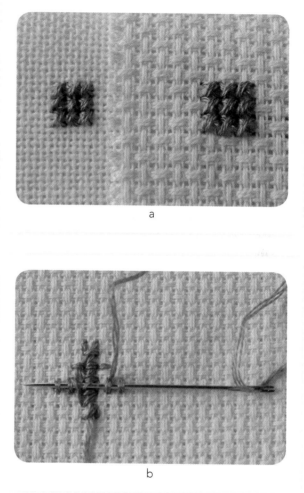

a

b

Menagerie at Midnight

Menagerie at Midnight

Pattern pages 125–128

Inspiration

While I wouldn't consider this work the simplest design in the book, it is the first cross stitch that I specifically designed to be very different from what I am familiar with when I think of cross stitch. There are so many extraordinarily beautiful examples of traditional cross-stitch samplers that, by and large, are set to a somewhat symmetrical layout. Sometimes they are in exact symmetry, which gives them a deceptively simple charm. The result seems to belie the amount of time it actually takes to complete them because the finished work is so quickly understandable.

With that in mind, I wanted to create a work that has balance but not symmetry, more like a painting might have balance. What I appreciate about traditional cross-stitch works is the awkward sense of perspective and scale that comes about simply through the process of rendering forms and creatures in a way that makes them recognizable but not detailed or too large. A peacock is nearly as large as a willow tree. A flower looks like it's been flattened in a book and is set in perpetual motion with just a few extra directional lines swirling about. To add a bit of drama and turn tradition a little on its head, I also chose to work the design on black rather than cream or white. My daughter Juliana also thinks this looks like candy and a computer game all at once, which makes it even better.

THREAD:
Anchor six-strand embroidery floss (use three strands)

COLORS:
29, 47, 50, 66, 89, 92, 148, 161, 167, 188, 256, 276, 289, 303, 340, 365, 400, 433, 870, 926, 1009, 1043

CLOTH:
Aida cloth, 11 count, black (at least 18" x 16")

STITCH COUNT:
137 stitches tall x 116 stitches wide

FINISHED SIZE:
Approximately 12 ½" tall x 10 ½" wide

PATTERN:
Pattern is broken into four quadrants that are labeled top left (A), top right (B), bottom left (C), and bottom right (D). Each has markings to ensure your correct orientation.

Notes

* When I first began this project, I didn't use a hoop since my Aida cloth was quite stiff. Eventually I did switch to a circular hoop because even though the fabric was firm enough to stitch across neatly without one, it was large enough that I didn't want it flopping around as I worked.

* By the time I got a lot of the work finished, I decided to try out a rolling wooden frame for the first time, which I really liked. This type of frame is best used on cloths that don't have to be pulled too tightly because they are stretched only in one direction and left open on the sides.

* Working on the black Aida cloth was a different sort of challenge than on a pale background. I definitely recommend working in good daylight, or splurging on a special light for needlework. I noticed a fun, albeit peculiar, little trick to working with black Aida cloth. One afternoon when I was wearing a cream-colored skirt that showed through the holes of the black cloth as I held it in my lap, I found that doing the work was so much easier! So I kept changing into that skirt when I worked on this design.

Voilà

From the beginning, I set out to treat this design as an artwork, so I decided to frame it. If you want to have it professionally framed, it can be beautiful but a little costly. If you'd like to frame the piece yourself, be sure to follow the finishing tips on page 122.

Four Tiles Collection

Four Tiles Collection

Inspiration

With the idea of instant gratification in mind, I designed these smaller works, or "tiles" as I think of them. Completely embracing the beauty of symmetry, these tile designs were further inspired by various painted ceramic tiles throughout the world. And just as tiles are set together in multiples, I thought it would be pretty to frame each of these unique beauties together as a grouping.

Common Materials for All Four Designs:

THREAD:
Anchor six-strand embroidery floss (use three strands)

CLOTH:
Aida cloth, 11 count, cream (at least 10" x 10" for each)

Spring Sprouting
Pattern page 129

COLORS:
29, 33, 47, 92, 97, 187, 279, 307, 333, 400, 433

STITCH COUNT:
57 stitches tall x 57 stitches wide

FINISHED SIZE:
Approximately 5 ¼" tall x 5 ¼" wide

Terrace Blooms
Pattern page 131

COLORS:
23, 29, 41, 89, 170, 187, 188, 203, 279, 280, 433, 1092

STITCH COUNT:
59 stitches tall x 59 stitches wide

FINISHED SIZE:
Approximately 5 ½" tall x 5 ½" wide

Spiritual Center
Pattern page 130

COLORS:
29, 47, 86, 89, 97, 161, 289, 316, 333, 365, 400, 433, 1030, 1092

STITCH COUNT:
59 stitches tall x 59 stitches wide

FINISHED SIZE:
Approximately 5 ½" tall x 5 ½" wide

Perpetual Motion
Pattern page 132

COLORS:
29, 167, 170, 279, 333, 365, 400, 433, 1030, 1043

STITCH COUNT:
59 stitches tall x 59 stitches wide

FINISHED SIZE:
Approximately 5 ½" tall x 5 ½" wide

Notes

* Working on a design that is symmetrical like this is easy, and I found myself referring to the work itself for where to stitch next as much I was referring to the chart.
* These works would also be beautiful combined on one piece of cloth.
* Because of their smaller scale, these designs are a nice opportunity to try out a second work in different shades of floss.

Voilà

As with Menagerie at Midnight, I chose to frame these works; refer to the framing tips on page 122. I thought displaying these works together would be a little interesting if I chose two different colors of the same frame style. Setting the same color frames at a diagonal sort of echoes the process of cross stitch itself.

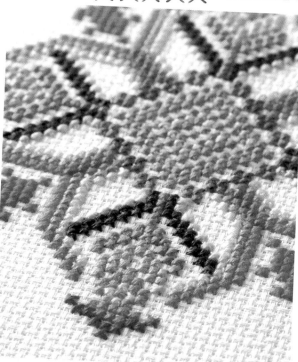

Border Beauties

belt

headband

table scarf

Trailing Kisses

Cupid Row

Waves of Plenty

skirt

tote

pillowcases

Border Beauties

Inspirations

I have to admit to going a little crazy with these border designs. With designs that are pretty small scale and easy to execute, it was hard not to picture each of them in different color combinations and also spreading across small or large expanses of cloth. I was very inspired by the gorgeous evenweave linen ribbon from France that I came across. It made quicker work of preparing these borders to apply to several projects because the edges are already beautifully finished. Evenweave ribbon is firm enough, so I didn't need to stretch it across any sort of hoop.

The nature and scale of these three border designs (Trailing Kisses, Cupid Row, and Waves of Plenty) make them adaptable to a huge variety of possibilities. Follow along with each design to see how I've sewn them into different projects. Feel free to do the same or mix up the designs and applications however you'd like.

Trailing Kisses Belt

Pattern page 133

THREAD:
Anchor six-strand embroidery floss (use two strands)

COLORS:
41, 297, 355, 1092

CLOTH:
Linen evenweave ribbon, 28 count, 1⅛" wide, cream, variable length

OTHER MATERIALS:
Ribbon (my own jacquard ribbons, 1" wide), double-sided lightweight interfacing, and 2 d-rings.

STITCH COUNT:
12 stitches tall x 18 stitches wide (each repeat)

FINISHED SIZE:
Approximately ⅞" tall x 1¼" wide (each repeat)

Notes

I repeated the Trailing Kisses pattern for about 30" to make a belt for Eleni. Once the stitching part was complete, I lightly fused the wrong side of the belt to the wrong side of some ribbon using double-sided fusible lightweight interfacing. I hemmed in one end, and then fed the other end through two d-rings before hemming.

Voilà

She said "Wow!" Eleni absolutely loves this belt and said she wants to wear it every day. Even better, she wants to try to make one herself. Now that's a nice finish!

Trailing Kisses Skirt Hem

Pattern page 133

THREAD:
Anchor six-strand embroidery floss (use two strands)

COLORS:
29, 187, 203, 333

CLOTH:
Linen evenweave ribbon, 28 count, 1⅛" wide, cream, variable length

STITCH COUNT:
12 stitches tall x 18 stitches wide (each repeat)

FINISHED SIZE:
Approximately ⅞" tall x 1¼" wide (each repeat)

Notes

* This border is continued for a length of about 40" so that it wraps all the way around this skirt hem for a pretty finish to a simple skirt.

* The skirt uses my own Flirting the Issue Skirt pattern, which is free on my website (http://annamariahorner.com/make). It's my girls' favorite skirt pattern.

Voilà

Using a thread the same color as the background of the evenweave ribbon lets the stitch work shine. Next time, I might try hand-stitching the border in place with floss for another detail.

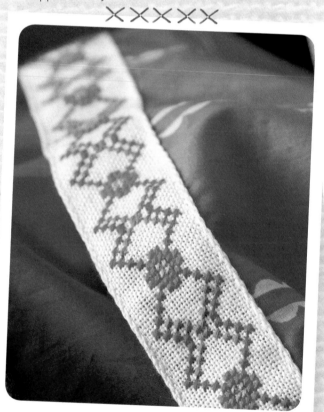

Cupid Row Headband

Pattern page 133

THREAD:
Anchor six-strand embroidery floss (use two strands)

COLORS:
29, 33, 41, 50, 66, 86, 89, 92, 147, 161, 170, 400, 433, 1035

CLOTH:
Linen evenweave ribbon, 28 count, 1⅛" wide, cream, about 12"

OTHER MATERIALS:
A premade fabric-covered headband from the craft store.

STITCH COUNT:
10 stitches tall x 123 stitches wide (each repeat)

FINISHED SIZE:
Approximately ¾" tall x 8 ¾" wide (each repeat)

Notes

* I designed Cupid Row around Valentine's Day but wanted to be sure the design could be worn all year if it was going to be included in clothing or accessories. So using colors in addition to pink and red really helps achieve that universal look.

Voilà

Since fully fabric headbands have a tendency to slip out (especially if you have fine hair like Isabela), we decided to use a finished fabric headband that we found at a craft store as a starting point. Attaching the border was as simple as whipstitching it at the edges and wrapping it around to the underside for stitching as the band begins to narrow toward the ends.

Cupid Row Tote

Pattern page 133

THREAD:
Anchor six-strand embroidery floss (use two strands)

COLORS:
29, 400, 433

CLOTH:
Linen evenweave ribbon, 28 count, 2 ¼" wide, beige

OTHER MATERIALS:
Your favorite tote sewing pattern or a store-bought tote.

STITCH COUNT:
10 stitches tall x 123 stitches wide (each repeat)

FINISHED SIZE:
Approximately ¾" tall x 8 ¾" wide (each repeat)

Notes

* I added the hearts-and-arrows border to about 16" of evenweave ribbon for a tote for me.
* I chose my floss colors to be slightly less sweet than on the headband and stitched them onto a wider ribbon. The effect on a simple tote is bold and graphic.
* My tote is made with black wool and lined with laminated cotton. You could just as easily sew a cross-stitched ribbon to a store-bought tote, either in the same direction I did, or as a border going around the top of the bag horizontally.

Voilà

To add the stitched border to a tote, apply the ribbon by machine or hand sewing to the front and back piece of your favorite bag pattern after you've cut those pieces out—before you've assembled the bag.

Waves of Plenty Table Scarf

Pattern page 134

THREAD:
Anchor six-strand embroidery floss (use two strands)

COLORS:
170 (2 skeins)

CLOTH:
Linen evenweave 28 count, cream (I used a 20" x 27" piece to create a 12" x 18" cloth)

OTHER MATERIALS:
Backing fabric in the same dimensions as your finished front piece.

STITCH COUNT:
22 stitches tall x 28 stitches wide (each repeat)

FINISHED SIZE:
Approximately 1½" tall x 2" wide (each repeat)

Notes

* The simple elegance of an extra layer underneath favorite dishes or vases echoes an air of humility and elevated living all at once.

* The striking two-color scheme for the table scarf honors my Yiayia (grandma) Eleni's memory and the beautiful two-color wool blankets that she hand-loomed for my family when I was growing up (see page 10).

* I layered two rows of the same border at each end of the cloth but staggered their positioning for variety in design.

* To scale the cloth how you'd like it to be, simply mark out the perimeter onto the evenweave cloth first with a water-soluble pen. Mark the center line from one end to the other also so that your design is symmetrical from one end to the other.

Voilà

Once the stitching is completed to the perimeter lines, trim the material within ½" of the line and sew right sides together with another piece of backing cloth using a ½" seam allowance and leaving an opening to turn through to the right side. Close the opening with an invisible hand stitch.

Waves of Plenty Pillowcase

Pattern page 134

THREAD:
Anchor six-strand embroidery floss (use two strands)

COLORS:
33, 41, 170, 187, 188, 238, 307, 355, 400, 1043, 1092

CLOTH:
Linen evenweave ribbon, 28 count, 2 ¼" wide, beige, ⅔ yard for each pillow

OTHER MATERIALS:
Any pillowcase you already have, or sew a new one.

STITCH COUNT:
22 stitches tall x 28 stitches wide (each repeat)

FINISHED SIZE:
Approximately 1½" tall x 2" wide (each repeat)

Notes

* I couldn't help trying out this beautiful border in a fuller palette of colors. As with so many projects, it's a great idea to use a favorite fabric for inspiration.

* My favorite part of designing needlework patterns is to create them in a way that complements my textile designs. Raindrop Poppies is one of my favorite fabrics! I created the design with the thought of raindrops on a window. And the way the stems sort of move and merge together reminds me of how streaks of rain will fall in line with one another on your car window as you speed along.

* While the final pillowcases were made from coordinating solid fabrics, they are piled together with other pillows made from my inspiration fabric.

Voilà

There are several ways to sew a lovely pillowcase, but to get your measurements right, just use one of your store-bought pillowcases as a guide. I sewed a nice wide solid border onto the open end of mine so that the stitched ribbon length would have a beautiful, bold frame to rest against. Completing this detailed cross-stitch border is time consuming, but the pillowcases are quite ready to become family heirlooms.

AlphaCute

AlphaCute

Pattern pages 135–136

Inspiration

How is it that hand-stitched letters are so cute? The style of this alphabet is somewhat schoolhouse like, which is very charming. One alphabet can go a long way, too! You can spell a name, a word, a phrase, or just the initials of a monogram. Applying a few or a lot of the letters on all sorts of objects would make a lovely baby gift.

THREAD:
Anchor six-strand embroidery floss (use two strands)

COLORS:
Every color!

CLOTH:
Aida cloth, 14 count, white (To make a whole alphabet of blocks, you'll need a few 20" x 27" cuts)

OTHER MATERIALS:
For each block, five squares of cotton fabric in your desired block size, heavy interfacing, fiberfill.

STITCH COUNT:
Varies from 27 stitches tall x 13 stitches wide to 59 stitches tall x 48 stitches wide

FINISHED SIZE:
Varies from approximately 2" tall x 1" wide to 4 ¼" tall x 3 ⅜" wide, depending on the letter

Notes

* You can just as easily include these stitched letters in a quilt block, as an ornament, or as the whole alphabet for a framed work.
* I chose to stitch the whole alphabet onto cloth squares and work them into some patchwork blocks. I marked off my evenweave cloth with either 4" or 5" squares, depending on the size of the letter, using a water-soluble pen. Then I centered each letter inside a 4" square to stitch.
* I also used some heavy interfacing squares to slide into each side of the sewn blocks before stuffing and sewing them closed, so that the sides would maintain a flat surface that is easier for stacking.

Voilà

I chose five lovely coordinating prints from my friend Denyse Schmidt's charming collection to patch together with the letter side for each three-dimensional block. I sewed four squares one to the next, side by side, using a ¼" seam allowance. Then I joined the first square in the row to the last one. With squares this small, I found it easier to sew the top and the bottom squares in place on the block by hand instead of by machine. In fact, with some of the blocks I decided to whipstitch all seams together by hand, which adds a nice detail. Once I had all but the last square in place, I set some squares of interfacing onto the wrong side of the block wall to keep them firm.

Name That Kid

Name That Kid

Pattern pages 135–136

Inspiration

I can be serious about my love for hand work but still poke fun at my own inability to quickly produce one of my children's names within a split second, right? And after six children (+ one husband, one dog, and one bird of blessed memory) it's perfectly acceptable to call each child by every other name in the family before verbally stumbling across their name, yes? If I could get everyone in the family to agree to just an initial on their front side, perhaps I would be helped.

There is no reason why you can't introduce your love of cross stitch to your love of crochet or knitting. Several handknit and crocheted materials can provide a nice surface for taking some extra big cross stitches with a large needle and your favorite yarn colors. But the Tunisian crochet stitch (which is sometimes referred to as the Afghan stitch) is particularly lovely because it creates a very even grid of cloth that is easy to make and therefore very simple to cross stitch onto. You might already have a favorite crochet pattern to make a sweater vest (or pillow too) for the little one in your life, so simply rework the pattern to include the Tunisian stitch at least on the bodice front. This will take a little swatch making to get your gauge right.

THREAD:
Rowan Pure Wool DK yarn and Anchor tapestry wool for the "r"

COLORS:
Earth (Rowan) and 8920 (Anchor)

CLOTH:
Crochet sweater created with Tunisian crochet stitch

OTHER MATERIALS:
Size 10 afghan crochet hook and a large-sized needle for sewing yarn.

STITCH COUNT:
Depends on letter; the "r" shown is 25 stitches tall x 22 stitches wide

FINISHED SIZE:
Depends on gauge of sweater material

PATTERN:
Use desired letter from AlphaCute pattern

Notes

* I can picture this little vest framed under glass someday in a bigger boy's room as a sweet childhood memory, or as a keepsake for his own family.

* Choosing high-contrast colors is perfect for silly little ones, but if you're making this project for an older child you might choose colors that are a little closer in value for a subtle look.

* Wait until after you've blocked the sweater front to sew your cross-stitch letter into place. Count out the perimeter of the letter in height and width stitches in order to center it on the sweater accordingly.

Voilà

Stitching the cross stitch onto the sweater uses all the
same techniques as regular cross stitching, but don't use
a hoop. Knot your yarn ends onto the wrong side
of the sweater.

✕ ✕ ✕ ✕ ✕

Crossing the Line

Crossing the Line

Inspirations

After having purchased a few items of clothing from my favorite stores, which have cross stitch included on them, I set out to figure out the best way to do this myself since the cross stich wasn't on evenweave cloth. I love the texture and charm of the cloths intended for cross stitch but didn't want to limit my cross-stitch designs to work only on woven cotton or linen.

After some research, I came across the marvelous wonder that is known as waste cloth or waste canvas. It's given that name because it is a temporary material that you layer over a non-evenweave material to provide a grid for making your cross stitches. (I suppose you could make needlepoint stitches as well.) After the design is stitched, you carefully discard the waste cloth by pulling the threads of them away one by one. There are also other varieties of waste cloth that will dissolve. I could have essentially chosen any fabric to sew a garment with, but for this project I specifically wanted to purchase a readymade garment. So my first job was to go shopping for some garments to stitch on, keeping in mind the fact that I would be spending a little time on these pieces; I wanted them to be affordable but not too cheaply made.

Merging Pathways Design

Pattern page 137

THREAD:
Anchor six-strand floss (use four strands)

COLORS:
29, 89, 92, 161, 188, 256, 433, 1030, 1043

CLOTH:
8.5 count waste cloth on store-bought woven blouse with zipper

STITCH COUNT:
64 stitches tall x 45 stitches wide

FINISHED SIZE:
7½" tall x 5¼" wide

Notes

* Most of my inspirations about how to design these cross-stitch works came about from the very clothing that I selected. The Merging Pathways design is perfectly suited to be placed on either side of an exposed zipper, but would work nicely at the bottom of a button placket that ends at the bust line as well.

* The following steps detail the process of using waste cloth for your cross-stitch project:

1 Be sure that your waste cloth has been trimmed to be a few inches larger in each direction than your final design dimensions.

2 Select the position on the fabric or garment where you would like to perform your stitching, and lightly mark the center point with fabric chalk.

3 Pin the waste cloth in place, aligning its center with your marked center. If you are applying the waste cloth to a finished garment, you might want to slide a book in between the front and back layers of the garment to prevent you from accidentally including an extra layer of fabric in your pinning.

4 With large stitches, hand baste the waste cloth into place, keeping its grid in line with the grain of the material, particularly if you are sewing at an edge or near something with a defined straight edge like a zipper or striped material.

5 Once the basting is complete, remove the pins and begin your design using the waste cloth as a guide for stitching.

6 After the cross-stitch work is complete, take care in removing the threads of the waste cloth one by one. Follow the directions provided with the waste cloth you purchased to be sure you are using the proper method.

- The waste canvas has a larger stitch size than most of the cross-stich projects, so I chose to stitch with four strands of cotton. I found the results to be perfect for the 8.5 count waste cloth.

- With the firm waste canvas basted to my fabric, I never need any type of hoop because the fabric is set firmly in place and easy to stitch.

Voilà

This project has such a stunning result for such a simple process. Once the work is complete, you might choose to fuse a lightweight woven interfacing onto the back side of your stitching work to make sure that the stitches aren't disturbed as the garment is worn or cared for. (It also might eliminate any itchiness.)

Long Way Home

Pattern page 137

THREAD:
Anchor six-strand floss (use all six strands)

COLORS:
50, 89

CLOTH:
8.5 count waste canvas on store-bought knit blouse

STITCH COUNT:
14 stitches tall x 116 stitches wide

FINISHED SIZE:
Approximately 1⅜" tall x 13⅝" wide

Notes

* I wasn't sure how it would turn out, but I wanted to try this pattern on a knit fabric. I was really pleased with the result.
* It did prove a good idea to keep the stitching design pretty simple. Just as a zigzag stitch with your sewing machine will allow a knit fabric to continue to stretch, I thought that a cross-stitch design with a zigzag formation would do the same.
* I chose to use six strands of floss for a chunky effect, although the X is slightly less pronounced because of this.
* Switching the colors from light pink to dark pink as the zigzag line crosses over white and black creates a really nice visual effect.

Voilà

Take extra care when placing your waste cloth onto a stripe. Keep the waste cloth grid in line with the stripes of the material so that your stitching can stay in line with them as well. Because of the minimal stitching, I decided to leave this piece without any sort of interfacing. This is so much more than a striped shirt now, and I feel tempted to turn a stripe into a plaid with X's next!

Needlepoint

I simply adore how the regular worked surface of a wool needlepoint feels under my fingertips. Its beauty and characteristics seem intended for such enjoyment. The heavier canvas and the wool yarns, which are traditionally married together in needlepoint, seem up to the task of a little more interaction, and so needlepoint ranks among the sturdiest of all needlework. For this reason, the pieces aren't too entirely delicate. Needlepoint is very often worked into interiors, not just as framed works but also in the form of pillows, cushions, and upholstery. I frequently hear my European friends refer to needlepoint as tapestry, and while true tapestry is woven on a vertical loom and not an open canvas, they do share similarities in their finished quality.

A great deal of technical information is available through many wonderful books that present the best way to perform every kind of needlepoint stitch ever created. These books also present a variety of additonal techniques for performing each of those stitches while keeping in mind the end use of the work. I frequently reference these technical texts, and relish in learning the intricacies of the craft. Within the context of this book, however, I am focused on arming you with enough information to complete the projects offered here and perhaps provide the inspiration to venture further should you so choose. So with that in mind, let's begin our needlepoint journey.

Common Materials and Tools

So many of the best needlepoint projects come in the form of kits that include wool for working the design onto a screen-printed canvas, or simply a hand-painted canvas, for which you would choose the wool yourself. While a hand-painted canvas can be very costly compared to a screen-printed version, this is usually because of how meticulously the canvas has been painted. Very often in screen-printed varieties, an intersection of canvas threads (where one stitch will occur) may have more than one color printed across it, leaving the stitcher to decide which color to use when stitching the design. This is not much of an inconvenience for the experienced stitcher; however, with most hand-painted canvases, the creators have taken care to apply the paint to the canvas so that there is no question which color yarn to use throughout the work. In other words, every intersection of canvas thread has been carefully painted with precision. If, however, you would like to build one of your own designs, paint one of your own canvases, or follow a counted work on a blank canvas, it is useful to get a handle on the available materials.

Needlepoint canvas or "mesh," like evenweave, is available in several count sizes or threads per inch. As the term *mesh* suggests, the material is very open compared to evenweave cloth, and the holes for stitching are more obvious and easier to see. There are several types of needlepoint canvas, but three in particular seem easier to find as blank canvas or as part of a kit. *Mono* canvas is a single-mesh canvas where each intersection is achieved by a single-warp and single-weft thread and woven in a typical fashion. It is suitable for a variety of stitches, though the intersections are secured with nothing more than the sizing that stiffens the canvas; as a result it may be the least stable canvas, as the threads could slip out of place when working on a piece over time. *Interlock* canvas is also single mesh; however, an additional smaller-warp thread has been twisted around the weft at each intersection, making the surface more rigid and secure. Finally, *Penelope* canvas is woven with two warps and two wefts at every intersection so that the stitcher can alternate between using larger stitches and splitting them into half-size stitches to achieve the finer detail commonly found in petit point.

All of the needlepoint projects in this book are made using interlock canvas, which I chose because it's easy to find and does not ravel easily when cut. It is also rigid enough that you could forego using a frame while you work. If you choose to use a frame, they are generally available in several sizes and two styles. A scroll frame secures the canvas from two sides that can continue to be rolled as you work, leaving only a small portion of the canvas visible for stitching. A four-sided frame is created from stretcher strips that you assemble. Along with a frame, there are also stands that can hold the frame so that you don't have to hold it with your hands. I am still experimenting with what I prefer, but I am finding that it depends on the size of the work. I don't mind holding a small canvas in my hands, but the larger it becomes, the more I would like it to be still and stable, keeping my hands free. Of course, you should experiment with and without frames, and hopefully my notes regarding frame choices for each project will be helpful.

While the needlepoint canvas you're about to work with seems rigid with no possibility of unraveling, it is still a great idea to wrap masking tape around the edges of your work before you begin. I found that I wanted the taped edges to stabilize the canvas as much as I wanted them to prevent the scratchy edges from irritating my forearms or snagging my clothes as I worked. Additionally, to prepare your canvas when following a charted work, it's a good idea to mark out your stitching area (by counting out the stitch size of the work) with a water-soluble pen around the perimeter.

Perhaps more than any other stitched art, needlepoint traditionally portrays images that are quite painterly, and therefore a certain degree of detail is desirable in the work. If you are designing your own needlepoint, this makes the thread count of the canvas you chose an important consideration for your work. A finer canvas—one with a higher thread count—will offer more stitches per inch and, therefore, more room for color gradations for shading and so forth. Each of the projects offered in this chapter will suggest a specific canvas thread count. Canvas is also available in a few colors, though not so diverse as cloth for cross stitch because you generally cover every bit of canvas when you make needlepoint.

While a few different types of wool yarns are typically used for needlepoint, you can also find several examples of finer petit point works made from cotton or silk floss.

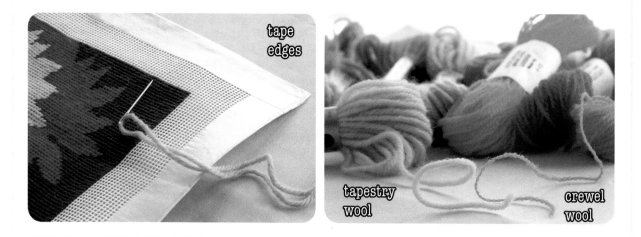

tape edges

tapestry wool

crewel wool

1

2

Most needlepoint kits come with a two-ply tapestry wool, which is perfect for many beautiful needlepoints and is very easy to use. This and other wools are also available in individual skeins. You can also use crewel wools, which are finer than standard tapestry wools and whose twisted ply is less apparent (plainly speaking, it's kind of fuzzier); this makes them well suited to blend a few strands of various colors together on your needle at the same time to achieve subtle shading. The thread count of a canvas and the relative size of the yarn's thickness are always important considerations for choosing both the type and the number of strands to use for your work. I've used both Anchor tapestry yarns and Appleton crewel yarns for my works in this chapter, so follow my notes with each project.

Simple, blunt-tipped tapestry needles will complete all needlepoint works perfectly, and they are available in a few sizes to correlate with various count sizes of canvas. You really shouldn't use a standard sharp-tipped needle for needlepoint because it can easily snag or poke through the canvas threads instead of smoothly nestling into the canvas holes as you stitch.

Stitch Know-how

Now that I've touched on everything but threading your needle and making that first stitch, I'll cover a few basics of how to begin and end your stitches, and the mechanics of the stitch styles that I used in my needlepoint projects.

The same cut-length rule of about 18" applies for needlepoint yarns as it does for other handwork. It might be even more important to stick to this rule for wool yarns than it is for cotton embroidery threads, because wool seems more likely to become threadbare if you use particularly long cuts. To thread your needle with these fluffier yarns: (1) Wrap the yarn around the tip of the needle to form a tight loop, slide it off, firmly held between your thumb and index finger; and (2) press the loop into the eye. This is easier than threading the cut end of the wool, which frays out rather quickly. Your needle will also tend to wear on the yarn if the eye is kept at the same position on the yarn length through much of the stitching. So it's a good idea to continually slide the needle's eye down the strand as you work so it's never in one spot for long.

To begin your first stitch, just as with cross stitch, enter first from the back, leave a tail of a few inches, and ensure that your first stitches are catching the tail. There are other methods of leaving the tail (either knotted or not) on the top surface, beginning your first stitch a few threads away, then cutting the tail later after it has been caught underneath by way of stitching; however, they all use the same concept. As you make stitches, you will always be entering canvas holes that are already or soon to

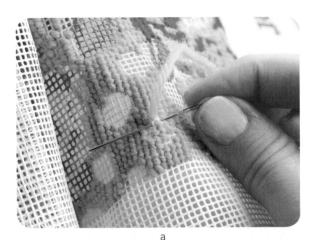

a

b

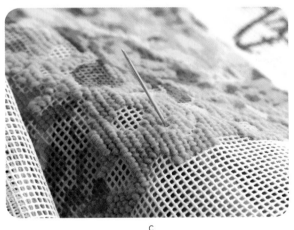

c

be occupied by other stitches since they pack in right next to one another on all sides. For this reason, it's important to take care as you enter the canvas, either from the front or the back, that the needle doesn't snag an existing stitch and, therefore, render uneven surfaces. Although this is very easy to avoid, it is worth mentioning.

With the actual stitch, as with every craft, the best style of making it is the one that feels most comfortable for you, and the one that gives you the results you desire. Performing the needlepoint stitch on canvas typically falls into one of two categories: *continuous* or *stabbing*. When making a continuous stitch, your dominant working hand is always on the top surface of the work, and you enter the needle down into the canvas and back up again in one motion before pulling through (a). While some stitchers might think this fashion warps the canvas, if it is comfortable and you can accommodate an appropriate tension, then go for it. I only find it possible to work this way without a frame, but I generally prefer it. And when I do work this way, I roll the excess canvas between myself and the space I am working right up to about an inch or two from my needle. When making a stabbing stitch, you enter the needle into the canvas from the top (b), pull through to the back then enter up to the top (c) and pull through again. Notice this places two pulls into the process. It generally takes longer than continuous stitching; however, it can be sped up by using a standing frame and keeping one hand working the top surface and the other working underneath. Experiment and find your favorite technique.

As with all my handwork, my stitching methods and my decision whether or not to use a frame are still evolving and tend to change depending on the scale of the project and where I am working on it. Once you've settled on either a continuous or stabbing method (whether with or without a frame) you should maintain that method throughout the work. The surface of standard tent-stitched needlepoint (which I'll detail in the next paragraph) tends to be much more regular than the surface of something like embroidery where different stitch styles create various

Patchwork Needlepoint Couch

✶ I collected several vintage needlepoints to include in this patchwork couch — they're simply patched w/ other scraps!

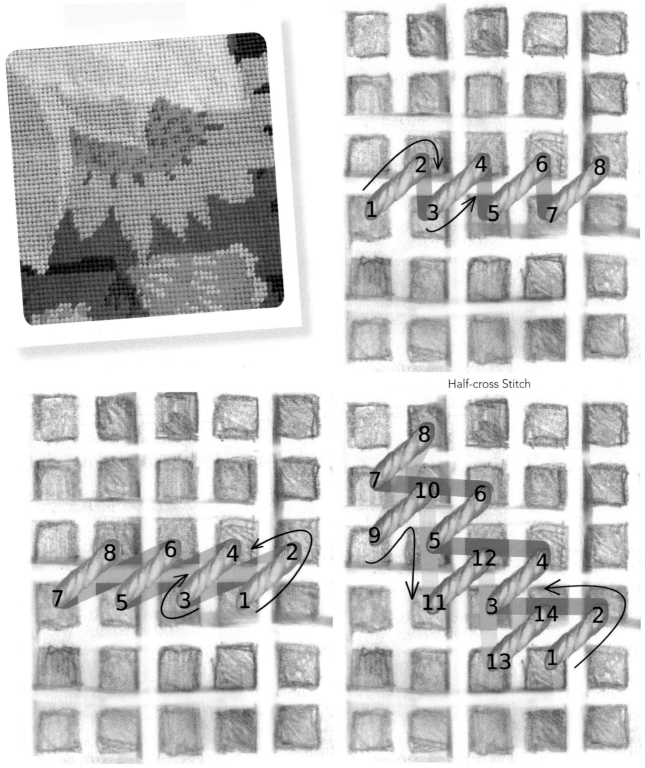

Half-cross Stitch

Continental Stitch

Basket Weave Stitch

textures. You may then realize that any inconsistencies in this very regular stitching are more obvious, and they usually arise out of irregular tension. The more practice you have, the more you will rely on a regular tautness to your work. Most of all be patient with yourself. Now let's learn some stitches!

Tent Stitch

Tent stitches are those standard needlepoint stitches that make a single diagonal stitch from one canvas hole to the adjacent hole on the diagonal. Within this category, there are three stitching methods. While each method may look the same from the front of the work, it's the back of the work that gives away the type of method; you will see that they each use a different amount of yarn to complete. The following descriptions are accompanied by color-coded illustrations where the pink stitches represent what is visible from the front of the canvas and the gold and blue stitches represent what is happening on the back of the canvas as you stitch. The numbers and arrows describe the sequence and direction of stitches.

HALF-CROSS STITCH

The first method is the half-cross stitch, which has a front side made up of diagonal stitches and a back side made up of vertical stitches. In other words, as shown in the diagram, a half-cross stitch is really nothing more than a whipstitch being made across the weft row of the canvas. You can also work half-cross stitches in vertical rows, and in this case the back of the work appears as horizontal stitches. By most accounts, this type of stitching, while very economical with your yarn, tends to warp the canvas once worked, and leaves very little yarn coverage on the back side. However, I would suggest that this is a good starting stitch for young people who would like to try needlepoint, as it is easy to pick up and works itself out very logically in every direction.

CONTINENTAL STITCH

The second method is the continental stitch, which actually has a diagonal finish on the back as well as the front; however, on the back it's with an angle that stretches across two warp threads as opposed to just one on the front. Just as with half-cross stitch, you can work this style in horizontal or vertical rows. Also for both half-cross and continental stitches, in order to always work from left to right or top to bottom (or whichever direction you choose), you simply turn the work when you get to the end of a row. Continental stitch is typically more desirable than half-cross because of the coverage it provides on the back of the work. While the stitches on the front are better defined than the whipstitch style of half-cross, it can also warp the canvas if you are not careful. Using a frame can help to eliminate this problem, and for the most part, blocking a work once it's complete can also correct most warping issues. (See blocking instructions on page 121.)

BASKET WEAVE STITCH

The third method, basket weave stitch, is the ideal needlepoint stitch because of the distinct surface it gives the work and because it causes the least amount of warping of all the tent stitch methods. It has good yarn coverage on the back of the work, which makes it ideal for items that will get a bit more use such as upholstered chairs and the like. If there is a drawback to this method, it is that it uses more yarn than the others, but when you consider the time given to your craft, it is a worthwhile investment. When looking at the back side of the basket weave stitch, it becomes apparent how it got its name. Basket weave always works itself in diagonal rows so there is never a need to turn the canvas as you work. It is similar to continental stitch in that when working either up or down, your needle is always passing straight under two canvas threads at a time, either vertical or horizontal depending on the direction you are heading. The numbered diagram of the stitching sequence helps to explain the process, but there is nothing like trying it out for yourself to reinforce the method.

Those with some needlepoint experience usually have a favorite method or a strong opinion about the superior qualities of one over another. The best approach is to try a few stitching methods, keeping in mind some of the pros and cons of each. Ideal stitch methods aside, working on a design involves filling in various shapes and sizes of color regions, and sometimes it becomes necessary to switch between methods to get yourself into and out of certain areas of the design or to get from one row to the next. For this reason, it's a good idea to familiarize yourself with all of the stitches, although you should try and stick mostly to one method in a single work. If you were left with nothing but yarn, needle, canvas, and no direction at all, you would eventually come to know these methods through practical experience.

Decorative Stitches

Beyond the basic diagonal stitches, there are an endless number of gorgeous needlepoint stitches that take these very simple materials and transform them into exquisite works. Whether they're worked with a single color or in color patterns, these styles often build the surface of the work in a way that provides additional layers of texture and interest. Some become so pictorial that they verge on looking more like an embroidered, crocheted, or knitted surface. But because they are still worked on a grid, the intricacies come from nothing more than adapting the length, sequence, or direction of the stitch, which means they are very simple to create. Use the diagrams on the following pages and their stitch sequences, which are numbered, to create some of my favorite decorative needlepoint stitches. Each stitch illustration has some yarn color variation to help point out the individual stitch units. There are further descriptions of each stitch style for clarification and inspiration.

Leaf Stitch

I really enjoy decorative stitches that are illustrative, as well as those that also nest beautifully into one another, such as this leaf stitch. Each unit works out to be ten stitches high and seven stitches wide so you can cover some ground pretty quickly with this stitch. A canvas made up of nothing but colorful rows of these leaves would be gorgeous. I've used it to accent the corners of the diamond pattern in my Nouveau Needle Cushion project.

Diamond Eyelet

The diamond eyelet took me a few tries before I liked how the stitches looked because there is quite a bit of yarn buildup with the sequence of this one. After about three of four tries, they started looking really uniform. There is no harm in having a sampling canvas nearby as you work on a new project to practice new stitches before including them in a final work. The short outline stitches around the diamond rays can be worked as single back stitches and are lovely when worked in a contrasting color to the rays.

Mosaic Stitch

The mosaic stitch is the smallest of the box-style stitches, as each unit is formed by only three (2-by-2-thread) diagonal stitches and covers only a 2 by 2–thread area of canvas. The center stitch is twice the length of the shorter single stitches on either side, and may need a little extra tension for it to appear as smooth. See the diagram on the next page for the sequence of working an area of mosaic stitch, with the contrast color is pointing out a single stitch unit. In the Nouveau Needle Cushion project, I created an area that uses this stitch method; however, it staggers the stitches vertically, which you'll see in the pattern's diagram.

Wicker Stitch

This stitch works itself very quickly and has such a charming, basket-like texture. It provides a lovely background element for almost any needlepoint work. Notice in the previous diagram of the wicker stitch that the end points of the three stitches in each unit tuck just under the side of another unit, so it is sometimes necessary to hold back the side stitch of the previously worked stitch with your thumb, in order to enter the canvas without snagging the already-worked stitches. With just a little practice, this process will become second nature.

Byzantine Stitch

I love this stair-step style because it is so visually dynamic and yet so simple. My original design for the Nouveau Needle Cushion did not include much of this stitch until I started working it. I became mesmerized by the graphic qualities of layering up several multicolored rows of these zigs and zags. A simple variation on the Byzantine stitch would be to include alternating rows of single needlepoint stitches (half-cross stitches) between the wider stair steps to provide some interest. This style is also referred to as the Jacquard stitch, and several combinations of the step width and height along with color changes can make for beautiful work.

Milanese Pinwheel

The moment I first saw this stitch design I instantly thought of quilt blocks, ceramic tiles, windmills, and other similarly striking and spinning design motifs. This pattern covers a lot of ground quickly and offers a wonderful opportunity to mix various colors together, as I did for the Star-Crossed Love clutch project. The illustration details the numerical stitching sequence of the pinwheel; however, the negative space that is created between the adjoining pinwheels could be filled in a variety of ways. The illustration simply shows a slanted stitch that fills the space, but you could employ any number of your favorites, including a simple tent stitch in this area.

Compensating Stitches

While all of these stitches will link beautifully to themselves one element after another, combining a few varieties of decorative stitches within the same work will often produce some small, odd spaces of empty canvas. This is where compensating stitches are called for in order to cover the canvas. If you are creating a symmetrical design such as in the Nouveau Needle Cushion project, keep in mind the overall effect that any regularly appearing compensating stitches will have on the final work before deciding on their color scheme. I tend to compensate with a tent stitch here and there as necessary and choose their color scheme based on supporting the overall composition of the work.

milanese pinwheel

Nouveau Needle Cushion

Nouveau Needle Cushion Pattern page 138

Inspiration

The creation of this project was almost entirely based on my desire to combine my favorite decorative stitches into one work—a sampler of sorts. So the overall design came about in an almost puzzle-like fashion, fitting the likes of one into the shape of another. I knew from the beginning that I would want to construct this square design into a little pillow to use as a needle cushion for my handwork needles. I have a ridiculous number of pincushions around the studio (and all over the house, too), but nothing that is devoted to my needles for needlework. I am therefore always digging through a variety of straight pins to find my needles. It might seem like a lot of effort to create something as utilitarian as a needle cushion that is destined to get a good amount of wear. However, I sort of relish in the idea of this beautiful little cushion sitting by my side as I work for years to come. Of course, should you be more inspired to present your piece differently, it could be left in its original state, as a flat work, or framed or sewn into a pillow or tote bag.

THREAD:

Anchor tapestry yarn

COLORS:

8424, 8434, 8440, 8458, 8524 (x2), 8712, 8920, 9154, 9284, 9790

CLOTH:

13" x 13" of white interlock needlepoint canvas (or more if you want to use a frame or hoop)

STITCH COUNT:

12 count

FINISHED SIZE:

Approximately 9" x 9" (if sewn into a needle cushion, finished size is about 6" x 6")

Notes

* Grid-style patterns that you follow for needlepoint or cross stitch typically offer blocks of color that each represent a single stitch on the canvas. For clarity's sake with this pattern, I've instead provided a chart that actually represents the style and direction of every stitch, and the grid shown behind the stitches represents the threads of the canvas.

* Also reference the stitch tutorials on page 58 for tips on making the stitches included in this project.

* Because this design joins several styles of stitches that don't always fit perfectly with each other, you might need to make compensating stitches (a simple tent stitch will do) here and there to cover any canvas that might be showing.

* Just like a hand-knit or crocheted sweater, your piece might require blocking to reshape it back to its original square form once complete. Follow the blocking instructions on page 121.

Voilà

Finishing this piece was really enjoyable. I folded back the excess canvas on each edge toward the wrong side and pressed it with my fingers all around. Then I simply turned back each of the four points to meet at the center back and safety-pinned opposing corners to one another to hold them in place. Joining the criss-cross seam on the back was as simple as whipstitching by beginning in the outer corner and passing the needle through the last worked rows on each side to stitch (as shown in the photo below). When doing this, you are working through the folded edge of the canvas. If you are not happy with the coverage of the wool over the canvas with one row of stitching, take a second pass over the top of the first row. Stuff the cushion with fiberfill before closing up the last ¼ of the criss-cross seam.

Star-Crossed Love

Star-Crossed Love

Inspiration

This project is such a hybrid of inspirations and disciplines. It has a stitch style borrowed from needlepoint, a yarn borrowed from crewel work, and a cloth most typically used for cross stitch. My desire to use the Milanese Pinwheel motif (page 61) was sparked around the same time that I was looking for a way to take inspiration from one of my mother's knit blankets. She started the blanket sometime in the mid-70s, and it took a visit from my grandmother from Greece late in the same decade to help her complete it. While the pattern style of my mother's knitted "blocks" is not exactly the same as the Milanese Pinwheel, it definitely inspired me to take a multi-colored approach to the design and to do so on a black background for a stunning effect.

My original plan with this design was to make a color change with every triangular section of every pinwheel, similar to the inspiration blanket shown on the next page. I only made it about halfway through one pinwheel before I decided that cutting and rethreading all those color changes was going to prevent me from enjoying this stitch. So instead I decided to let each pinwheel be a different color and the result is gorgeous. To add further interest and make it a little more top shelf, after the pinwheels were complete, I decided to needle some simple running stitches of gold into to the open areas between pinwheels using the natural threads of the Aida cloth to guide my stitches. Of course, it added a little time to the project, but also a great deal of beauty.

THREAD:
Appleton crewel wool (three strands) and gold metallic embroidery thread (four strands)

COLORS:
One skein each of 155, 311, 338, 435, 475, 486, 801, 944

CLOTH:
Black cotton Aida cloth (approximately 10" x 14", larger if you'd like to work with a frame or hoop)

STITCH COUNT:
11 count

OTHER MATERIALS:
12" zipper, ¼ yard of black woven fusible interfacing, ¼ yard of fabric for clutch back (or 8" x 12" scrap), and ⅓ yard of fabric for clutch lining (or 13" x 12" scrap).

FINISHED SIZE:
Approximately 6" x 10"

Notes

* Using the layout and stitching sequence for the Milanese Pinwheel on page 61, I made the design 6 full pinwheels wide and 3½ pinwheels tall, alternating color here and there as I went.

* I stitched this design from the center out. The Aida cloth I used was firm enough that I didn't need a hoop or frame. The layout of this motif and the way the pinwheels link together cause the pinwheels to stack one onto another across the pattern, so that the whole group of them lean at a slight angle once complete.

* After the pinwheels were complete, I drew a perimeter around them, ½" away from their edges, to mark my seam allowance edge for creating the clutch. I then made the gold stitches, keeping them about ¼" away from that drawn line, so that I would never be cutting through any stitching once I prepared to assemble the clutch.

Once the gold stitching was complete, I steam-pressed a lightweight black woven fusible interfacing (a little larger than my drawn perimeter line) onto the wrong side of the stitched Aida. I carefully cut the Aida on the drawn line around the perimeter, and then cut a back piece for the clutch in the same dimensions.

To create a sewn clutch using the stitched Aida piece, follow these steps:

1 With right sides together and using a ½" seam allowance, sew the Aida piece to the clutch back along the long bottom edge only. Press the seam open.

2 Use the joined outer pieces of the clutch as a pattern to cut one lining piece in the same dimensions.

3 Lay the zipper right side down along the top edge of the right side of the Aida piece, letting the head and tail of the zipper extend past each side edge of the Aida. Lay the lining piece right side down on top and in line with the joined outer pieces, thereby sandwiching the zipper in between the outer clutch and lining pieces. Pin through both layers and the zipper, and use the zipper foot on your machine to join all layers together along the top edge with a ⅜" seam allowance (or whatever seam allowance comfortably catches all layers and stays clear of sewing over the pinwheels).

4 Reach in for the unsewn edge of the zipper and pull it over to align it with the top edge of the clutch back, and then again sandwich it between the remaining top edge of the lining. Keeping other layers clear, pin it in place and sew as you did in Step 3.

5 Pull the inner and outer layers apart from each other. Fold the lining layer so that its right sides are against themselves, and the right sides of the front and back clutch are against themselves. Slide the zipper head into the center of the bag and keep the zipper tape edges folded down towards the outer bag. (Also keep the separated teeth in line with one another now that the zipper head is in the center.)

Inspiration blanket

6 Sew the front and back of the clutch together on one side using a ½" seam allowance and continue carefully across the zipper to also sew the lining to itself on the same side, all in the same pass. (You might want to use the flywheel on your machine to sew manually over the zipper intersection.)

7 Repeat Step 6 on the other side but stop your sewing pass about 4" from the folded bottom edge of the lining and backstitch. This leaves an opening for you to pull the bag through to the right side.

8 Carefully trim off the excess zipper between the teeth on both ends with some heavy-duty scissors, and then reach through the opening left in the lining to pull the clutch through to the right side and poke out your corners neatly.

9 Fold the unsewn edges of the lining toward their wrong sides by ½", and then machine-sew it closed with a topstitch. Situate the lining down into the outer clutch to complete it. If you want to press the finished piece, do not directly touch the wool with your iron; place a muslin cloth over it when pressing to protect it.

Voilà

The construction of this bag is straightforward, but the design of the stitching is so sophisticated that I count it as my dressiest clutch, perfect for a formal event or anywhere. To add interest and fun. I created a pompom with leftover yarns (including the metallic threads!) to use for a zipper pull. I braided another section of yarn, looped it through the zipper tab, knotted its ends together, and secured it to the pompom with some whipstitching that is hidden in the fluffiness.

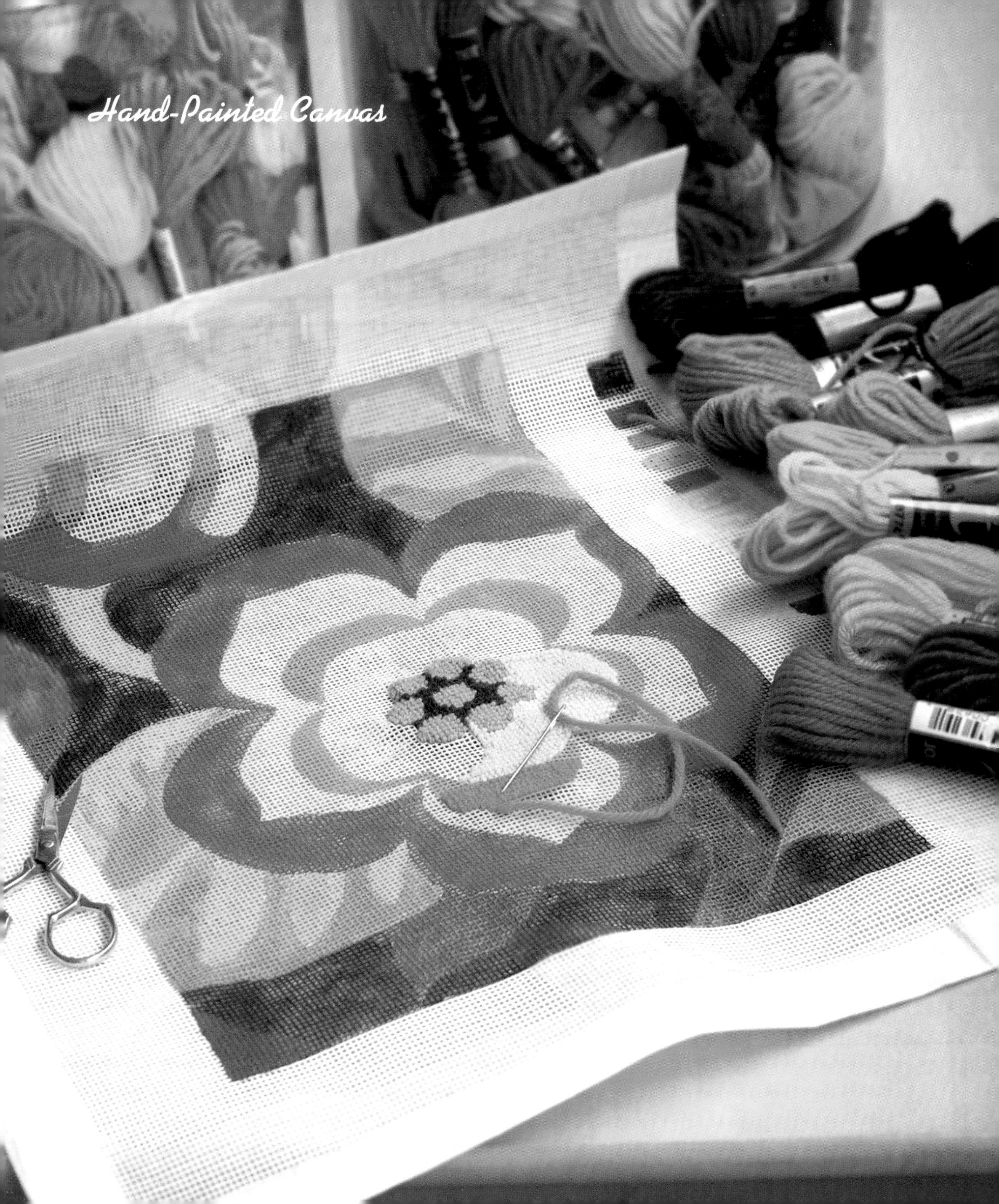
Hand-Painted Canvas

Hand-Painted Canvas

Inspiration

After having some experience with creating needlepoint using several methods and materials, I've realized how much I enjoy making my own designs, but I also really appreciate having a colored canvas to work from, which saves me from counting and following a separate grid pattern. Because I'm trained as a painter and have been working much of my life in textiles, painting my own work to be finished with stitching sits right at the middle of my two loves. It was an exciting and empowering project—empowering because the materials to complete it are so readily available, the process is pretty painless and immediate, and it saves a great deal of money. While the beginning of this project involves your own imagination, you could also use some favorite art or fabrics to inspire your design. Follow along with my notes for tips on making your own hand-painted needlepoint canvas.

MATERIALS:

White interlock needlepoint canvas

Acrylic paints (either artist tubes to be mixed with water or craft bottles to use as is)

Various artist brushes

Masking tape

Pencil

Paper, tracing paper

Craft scissors

Desired yarn colors

Wax paper

Tapestry needle

Notes

* Whether you begin with a full-color drawing from your computer, fine artwork that you want to see in stitches, or a simple line drawing from your sketchbook, you'll need to create a line drawing at your desired scale that separates regions of color. Then it might be helpful to make a few copies of your line drawing and start coloring like a coloring book, playing out a few color schemes with crayons, colored pencils, or markers. This process may end up enhancing your sketch, so retrace a new final version if necessary.

* I chose a simple floral drawing that I had done with a fairly limited assortment of just ten colors. Use the colored version of your sketch as a guide to selecting colors of wool for making the needlepoint. I think it's wise to figure out the wool colors you want to use first and then buy the paints to match. This is easier than finding wool to match your paints (so take your wools with you when you shop for paint).

1 To prepare the canvas for drawing and painting, I first cut the canvas 4 inches larger in each direction than my drawing (so a 9" x 12" drawing would require a 13" x 16" canvas). Needlepoint canvas is open and easy to see through, so you can treat it like tracing paper over your final line drawing.

2 Tape the drawing to the table to hold it in place. Center the canvas over it, and then trace out the perimeter of the drawing onto the canvas with a pencil. **Note:** *It is important to make the perimeter outline fall in line with the canvas threads, so that your final design will sit squarely on the canvas.* Secure the canvas to the table in a few spots with tape to avoid shifting, and begin to trace the line drawing from the paper onto the canvas using a pencil.

3 Once the drawing is complete, remove the paper line drawing from underneath the canvas, and lay wax paper in its place to protect your tabletop. Place a border of masking tape onto the canvas around the perimeter of the drawing to ensure a clean painted edge.

4 Use your colored version of the design to guide your painting process. I didn't start with a colored version but simply color-coded sections of my line drawing to guide where to paint each color. The consistency of paint that I found to work the best is similar to a creamy salad dressing. So whether you achieve that with bottled craft paints, or by mixing water with acrylic paints from a tube, this texture will spread well without getting too thick or too watery. The goal is to completely saturate the canvas with color but avoid clogging the canvas holes.

5 As you work, you may want to paint little swatches of color to the side so that you can later tie a sample of wool through each swatch to keep your colors in order.

6 Once the painting is complete, carefully lift the work off the wax paper (it will probably stick a little) and pin it somewhere to dry. If you cannot finish the work all in one sitting, you should still lift it off of the wax paper between working sessions so that it doesn't adhere to the paper when dry. Don't worry if some of the canvas holes become clogged. When the paint is still a little wet, you can actually blow through holes to remove the paint, or once dry you can poke with a tapestry needle to clear for stitching.

7 Once your painting is complete, remove the tape from around the perimeter of the painted design and discard it. Before stitching, wrap tape around the edges of the needlepoint canvas as suggested on page 52.

Voilà

I "kitted" this project for myself once it was dry and ready to stitch by putting all my wool for it into a sealed plastic bag with the canvas rolled up. To make sure you have enough wool for your project, keep in mind which method of tent stitch you will use (the tent stitch tutorial is on page 57). Each skein of Anchor tapestry wool is about eight yards. Estimating coverage per yard can vary due to stitch tension, canvas count, color changes, and so on. It might be helpful to measure out a length of yarn, and work up your desired stitch style on a scrap piece of canvas to help you make an educated guess of how much yarn you will need.

Free
Works

The Free Works section of projects is devoted to the two forms of needlework that I would classify as "free style." The word *free* is used because the scale and direction of every stitch is simply guided by the stitch style you have chosen and your particular method of making it. It is not, however, guided by any sort of regularity in the weave or count of the material as is the case for counted works like cross stitch and needlepoint. It rather follows a pattern of line work that has first been transferred to the cloth. The two disciplines of freestyle work and therefore projects that I'll be sharing in this section are embroidery and crewel work.

Technically, the term *embroidery* can describe all of the disciplines offered in this book (and then some), as the needlecraft of embroidery really refers to any decorative stitching on cloth. However, for many, including myself, the word has come to mean a freeform style of decorative stitching that usually employs certain types of cotton or silk floss worked onto a cotton or linen material. Conversely, crewel work has—since its beginnings—almost exclusively referred to decorative stitching performed with wool and most often on a linen surface, particularly linen twill.

The two disciplines are therefore distinguished from one another based simply on the materials used in each. With further investigation, you will find subtle differences among the tools used in each needlecraft, as well as which tools have been refined to be most suitable for the given materials. These differences aside, embroidery and crewel share many common stitch styles and also similar techniques for transferring a pattern onto cloth. Practically any stitch style or transfer method you are familiar with in embroidery can be applied to crewel, and the reverse is true as well. A favorite pattern that you've created in crewel can just as easily be adapted and created in embroidery by simply changing out the materials. Both disciplines are similar to cross stitch in that the surface of the material that has been stitched on will show itself between the design elements, so the material's color and texture are a consideration in the overall design of a piece. For this reason, embroidery and crewel work motifs can be applied to a myriad of finished works such as clothing, accessories, bedding, and artwork.

As with all of the needlework categories shared in this book, several embroidery and crewel patterns and kits are available for purchase to get you started. These patterns might be offered as digital downloads, paper printouts, or even iron-on transfers but all begin with simple line drawings that need to be transferred or traced onto cloth. Once re-created on your material, that line work will provide a field map for you to perform your stitches. Additionally, color guides and stitch guides are sometimes included with purchased patterns, to instruct you where to change thread colors and which stitch styles are used in different areas of the work. All of these variables are left up to you to change around and tweak as you wish (free style, remember?).

Keeping in mind that line work is the primary foundation for embroidery and crewel, it may become obvious that developing your own designs for stitching is pretty simple and can be born from numerous inspirational sources. Just as I went through several forms of inspiration for developing counted designs in the Grid Works section, you can follow some of the same starting points for creating line work for embroidery and crewel. However, arriving at a simple line drawing for a pattern can be simpler than making a full grid for counted works. Imagery found in artwork, photographs, wallpaper, fabric, vintage materials, coloring books, clip art, and so forth can all be reworked into line drawings for embroidery and crewel. Your own drawings, your children's drawings, or, if you're handy on the computer, a digital drawing can all form the basis for a gorgeous design. Why limit your stitching to artwork alone? There are several beautiful ways to incorporate print or cursive handwritten words or computer-printed text into your stitching as well.

Methods for Transferring Line Work

While you can certainly draw freestyle directly onto cloth before beginning to stitch, you will more likely transfer a design from paper that you've either developed and completed yourself, or purchased in a finished state. The various methods for transferring your line drawings onto cloth rest in the tools that you use, and there are now more to choose from than ever. I've made a list of transfer tools and processes, with brief descriptions of how to carry them out and scenarios where that method would be either necessary or desirable. The projects in the following two chapters refer back to some of these transfer methods.

Tracing Paper

You should have tracing paper at your fingertips in your craft and sewing room because it's an indispensable material with so many uses. You can use tracing paper to trace over a sketch that you've started and turn it into a final line drawing to use as a pattern. In fact if you'd rather not tear the perforated pattern pages out of this book, you could instead first trace the lines using tracing paper and then use the redrawn pattern with your light table or taped onto a window to trace onto your material with a water-soluble pen or pencil. You can do the very same thing with a favorite iron-on transfer pattern so that you are sure to always have a copy of it before it's all ironed out. The other great thing about having a design on tracing paper is that it's equally useful as a pattern if you flip it to the reverse side since the paper is so transparent.

Water-Soluble Pen

I often use a water-soluble pen. As long as the material that you are drawing onto is light enough to see through at a light table or a window, using a water-soluble pen is a perfect solution for tracing line work. A simple spritz with a water bottle here and there, or even a dab of water from a small, clean paint brush, can dissolve any visible lines after your work has been stitched. There are several colors available, and you can choose whichever will show up best on the particular fabric you are using. There are varieties of marking pencils as well, and some that will disappear with heat. In addition to reading the manufacturer's instructions with any drawing tool that you use, the most important consideration is whether the way you want your material to be handled is compatible with the recommended method for making marks disappear from your material.

Fine Pencils

In many cases, a fine-leaded pencil or mechanical pencil is perfectly suitable for use directly on the fabric you will be stitching. The line is so fine, especially if you use an HB pencil or a mechanical pencil with a 0.7mm lead, that it seldom shows from underneath, even with the most sparse stitching. A fine pencil is recommended when you want a very fine line, instead of the sometimes wider lines created by water-soluble or transfer pens and pencils. Keep in mind that the water-soluble pens and pencils mentioned previously might be more suitable for drawing freeform right onto the fabric, because it's easy to change lines as you see fit by making them disappear and redrawing them. With pencil lines that won't disappear, you want to be sure about your drawings to prevent having to erase any lines, and therefore possibly compromise the surface of your material with rubbing. (There are some "erasable" fabric pencils in the marketplace, but I am always hesitant to work with a tool that might have me roughing up the surface of my fabric.) Though you probably have #2 pencils on hand, you would only want to use these lightly and if they are kept nice and sharp as you work.

Heat-Transfer Pencils and Pens

In many ways, a pencil or pen that can draw a line onto paper and then be ironed onto a cloth surface seems to fulfill several transferring needs for the needlework enthusiast. There are some considerations when using these products, however; the first is making sure that your particular fabric can take the high-heat settings necessary to make the transfer work well. Also, the lines that will be transferred onto the fabric will be permanent, so you should be sure that the stitching style that you use covers the line work. For that reason, you may want to leave out small details in the pattern design.

From what I've noticed, lines from heat-transfer pencils and pens can sometimes appear more faintly than you might want, and also a little thicker than you might be happy with. Getting the material warm with an iron first can help to prepare it to accept the transfer ink a little better, and keeping the drawn line as thin as possible can also help to keep the lines crisp once transferred. Because you are ironing these designs into place, just as with a purchased iron-on transfer, be sure that your design is drawn in the reverse so that the design is oriented correctly once it appears on fabric.

With regard to the paper used with the transfer pens and pencils, make sure it won't discolor your material as your iron heats it up against the material. In general, this means you should only use acid-free papers or perhaps consider purchasing some specialty heat-transfer paper. As with all tools, test it out on a scrap of the fabric you will use to be sure that you'll get the results you want.

Transfer Papers

I have very fond memories of playing with sets of carbon paper out of my parents' desk drawer as a kid. Transfer paper involves a similar process of laying the color side of the paper down against the material, then laying your pattern on top of that, facing you, before you use a stylus (pencil, pen, or tracing tool) to draw over your design, applying enough pressure to force lines of transfer ink onto your cloth.

The papers come in a variety of colors to show up on various shades of fabric, and some varieties wash out as well. This is a good method if your fabric is too dark, printed, or too thick to see through on a light table. The only drawback to this method is that you have two sheets of paper laid over your fabric instead of having your fabric on top, or visible through vellum, and so you'll need to take extra care to position your drawing correctly on the fabric. I used transfer paper to transfer the design for the Loves Me Bouquet project, which took such a long time to complete that the transfer lines started to fade after a few weeks. They didn't go away so much that I couldn't see them well enough to redraw. However, I did have to redraw with a water-soluble pen because I would never be able to re-create the exact registration that I had between all the layers when I first used the transfer paper. Fading lines are a good thing because they won't show up after your work is complete, but it seems they are best suited for a smaller and therefore quicker project.

Prick and Pounce

This method is actually centuries old and some form of the process has spanned across embroidery, tailoring, oil painting, and even back to very early fresco painting. Vermeer himself used this method in the seventeenth century to transfer his drawings from paper onto canvas in preparation for painting. A drawing is first made on a vellum paper (which is similar to tracing paper but smoother and more durable) and then a sharp instrument called a *pricker* (a needle or awl would work, too) is used to poke tiny holes into the vellum about every ⅛" or so along the lines of the drawing. The pricked paper is then laid over whichever surface one will sew (or paint) onto, and a fine dust made up of various materials such as cuttlefish bone or charcoal is "pounced" over the drawn lines, forcing the dust through the pricked holes and thereby transferring the design onto the surface underneath. The actual pouncer is a fabric pouch, or soft brush-style tool that has been either filled with the colored dust or dipped into it. There are specific sets of tools that can be purchased to perform this process, although there are homemade varieties you can find through a little research that can do the job as well.

After the dusty dots have appeared on the material, the next step is generally to paint or draw very fine lines to connect the dots with either watercolor paint or fine pencils. It would be ideal to take even greater care to do this in shades that coordinate with the planned stitch work. After you finish connecting the dots and the lines are in their final form, you can bang and flick the dust off of the surface of the material and then use a small baby brush to remove any residual dust.

Seem like a lot of trouble? While the process involves many tools, the main appeal of this method is that you might be using a material for your stitching that is either too dark or too thick to see through even at a light table, or the surface of the material is either plush or irregular, such as velveteen or wool, and would not take a transfer ink or pencil well. I chose to use this process for my Garden Geometry project on page 118 because I wanted to experience the process of such an old method. It was pretty laborious but very enjoyable. While I made some adaptations to the process for the sake of convenience and saving some money, I learned something new, which was very gratifying.

Basting

When you have a project that you will be spending a good amount of time on, or one that no transfer method of heat, or ink, or dust seems to suit, you can simply sketch your design onto the fabric surface with needle and thread. To do this, use a transparent, lightweight interfacing to draw your design onto first (which you can trace through easily from the original pattern). Then simply position the interfacing over the cloth, and pin through both layers around the perimeter, well outside of the drawn area. Use a hoop if you have room to, and then hand-baste simple running stitches along the lines of the drawing with needle and thread. If you are handy with the free-motion stitch setting on your sewing machine, you can try this out on your machine as well.

Once the basting is complete, simply tear away the interfacing, taking care to keep your basting stitches intact. There is interfacing that is specifically designed to tear away after embroidery. Whichever interfacing you choose to try this method with, test it out first on scrap material. Once your decorative stitching is complete, if there are any visible basting lines, carefully clip and tug them out using curved embroidery scissors and curved tweezers.

Every time I try a new tool or process for transferring, I get very excited and convince myself that it will become my new favorite way to redraw designs onto fabric. For many, transferring the design happens to be the least enjoyable part of embroidery or crewel work. Luckily, most of these tools are easy to find and pretty affordable, so I would encourage you to play around and find what suits your project best. Anything that gets you to the more relaxing stitching sooner counts as worth the research and tinkering to me.

Embroidery

Perhaps it's becoming obvious after reading the introduction to the Free Works section that embroidery can essentially be worked onto any material as long as the material can take a needle and thread. But to give you a starting point for what might seem like an overwhelming art form full of possibilities, I will share some of the basic materials and tools you can use in your embroidery, and go over a sampling of stitch styles that I've chosen to use in this book's projects.

Common Materials and Tools

Since you don't have to restrict the cloth used in embroidery to specific materials by thread count or a woven style as I did for the Grid Works section, you can simply let the end product guide your choices for selecting materials and colors. Because embroidery is so adaptable across so many materials, it is a welcome embellishment to your machine-sewn goods such as clothing, linens, accessories, quilts, soft toys, and so much more. Not to mention many store-bought items that can be transformed with some charming vignettes of embroidery. It is traditional, of course, to also make embroidered works for the sole purpose of framing and enjoying as works of art for years to come (see the framing tips on page 122).

I have chosen to embroider mostly onto solid quilting cottons, solid linen, and printed cottons, but I have also worked designs onto wool and cotton jersey knits. Sometimes I even embroider onto evenweave linen or cotton that is suitable for cross stitch simply because I like the texture (see the Letters Home project on page 112, which is actually crewel work but has the same applied theory). Once you are comfortable with some favorite stitch styles, embroidery offers a wonderful opportunity to experiment with endless combinations of thread and material, keeping color and density of stitching in mind. For instance, if you know that you will be creating some very heavy stitch work, you might want to make sure that your chosen material is tightly woven and durable enough to handle it well. Materials that are particularly gauze-y and lightweight might risk being overworked, with the needle causing gaping holes, or having the threads appear to cross from one section of the work to another on the back side of the fabric.

Most importantly, don't ever rule out a material for embroidery until you've given it a try. Sometimes just changing floss, needle varieties, or stitch styles can make even embroidering on a length of lace trim a lovely possibility. With all of that freedom in mind, it is a good idea to also consider the content of your material and how compatible it is with the content of your floss in terms of how to care for each. For that reason, I often choose natural materials that would have the same care recommendations as my cotton floss (more about floss in a moment).

Are you making a blouse and planning to embroider the yoke or sleeves? Or are you making a skirt on which you would like to see embroidery dance all around the hemline? Simply choose the materials you would want for sewing that project anyway, as I did for the Daylight Fading project (page 89). When I'm going to be combining embroidery work into a machine-sewn item, I tend to work on the embroidery first. To plan this stitching into your sewing patterns, first trace out the pattern piece onto cloth, and work the stitching in your desired position before cutting the material to include in your sewing construction steps.

Be sure to keep your eventual seam allowance recommendations for constructing the garment in mind, and keep your stitching well away from this perimeter. Stitching your design onto a pattern piece that has been drawn onto a larger piece of cloth will ensure that you have enough room for using a hoop and will not worry about wearing out the edges of an already-cut pattern piece. If you're not sure what your embroidered work might end up as, it's a good idea to keep your options open and work the stitching on an ample-sized cloth.

Once your embroidery for a garment is complete, I recommend fusing some lightweight woven interfacing onto the back side of the work to keep the threads from getting snagged as you sew the item. The interfacing will also protect the work from wear once your garment is complete and in use. When you press embroidery (whether to fuse interfacing or just to freshen it up), be sure to place the right side of the embroidered work down on a plush towel before pressing from the wrong side with the iron. This will prevent the iron from flattening out your stitches.

I am a fan of using Anchor six-stand embroidery floss, which is available in over 400 colors. For the sake of disclosure, I work with the Anchor company to develop palette collections of floss and other threads, but I find their products to be luminous and high quality. I do not, however, get hung up on brands. So if you have a favorite brand and want to translate the color suggestions I've offered in my projects into that brand's color chart, there are several online resources that will do that for you. With the six-strand floss, you can separate the strands easily from one another and create a thread that varies in thickness for a variety of stitched textures.

I also enjoy using Anchor Pearl Cotton in some of my embroidery projects, which is different from the strand variety in that it is a two-ply twisted thread available in a handful of sizes as well as different thicknesses. You do not separate these threads, but use them whole. I mostly use a pearl cotton size 8 for my hand-quilting, which is pretty much in the middle of the thickness offerings (lower numbers being thicker and higher numbers being thinner). I also use Anchor Pearl Cotton in a variety of jewelry, edging and miniature crochet techniques (see page 92).

Other embroidery tools are very straightforward and readily available. A simple range of embroidery needle sizes, a few sizes of hoops, either wooden or plastic, and some embroidery snips can sit by your side as reliable companions while you stitch away. I keep a good variety of needles on hand—shorter, longer, smaller eye, larger eye—all to serve whatever stitch I am performing and the number of strands of thread I might be fitting through the eye. For instance, I don't want to use a long needle to make French Knots because I find it a lot easier to use a shorter one to wrap the threads around as I form the knots. I also don't want to use a needle with an eye larger than what will accommodate my threads because the goal is to make the smallest possible hole in the material while keeping the threading manageable. There are several varieties of scissors, but I tend to stick to basic embroidery snips, though I really appreciate the curved variety that do a better job at staying away from neighboring threads on the back when I snip a finished length close to the working surface.

Stitch Know-how

Threading your needle and getting started on the first stitch as well as finishing off the tail end of a thread is pretty much the same as recommended for cross stitch on page 26. However, particularly with embroidery I see no harm in starting out with a knot on the back of your work if you want to, rather than finding a way to catch your tail as you begin. Catching your tail is sometimes a challenge and takes your focus away from performing beautiful stitches. This to me seems not worth the fuss when you consider that embroidery typically builds up a variety of textures and surface thicknesses so that any tiny bump of a knot on the back of your work will have little to no consequence in the end. Once you have a bit of the surface worked, it is simple to find an entry into the back of the work, passing your needle underneath some neighboring stitches, without having to tie a knot.

Before I move on to the various stitch styles, keep in mind that all of the stitches shown provide a few basic functions in the design of an overall work. In cross stitch or with tent stitch in needlepoint, every stitch provides an equal amount of appeal and texture, so it's only the color that really dictates the design elements. Embroidery stitches provide variety on several levels, such as color, density, and texture. Some stitches are very linear by nature and prove perfect outlining options, such as back stitch, stem stitch, split stitch, laced running stitch, and chain stitch. That's not to say that certain densities and arrangements of these styles couldn't also act as fill stitches. Common fill stitches that serve well to cover some larger expanses of space with various textures are satin stitch, seed stitch, and various woven stitches. There are some stitches whose best attributes are to provide a smattering of texture, such as French knots, lazy daisy, bullion, and eyelet stitches. I mention all this to help you become accustomed to the nature of these stitches as design components—not to limit how you can use them. Let's get to making some of these beauties, shall we?

Back Stitch

1. Make a stitch

2. Begin the next one stitch length away, and then come back to meet the first

3. Continue as shown to create a continuous line of stitching

Stem Stitch

1. Make a stitch, do not pull through all the way, and then enter again half of a stitch length back

2. Repeat Step 1, keeping all your entry points on the marked line

3. Continuing in this manner will form a ropelike length of stitches

Split Stitch

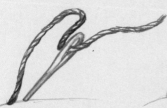  

1. Make a stitch

2. Enter the next stitch by coming up through the first to "split" it

3. Continue to split stitch for a continuous line. This stitch can also be used to fill.

laced running stitch & double laced running stitch

1. After making a simple running stitch or a back stitch, simply enter underneath a stitch with a new thread and weave through the top edge of one stitch and then through the bottom edge of the next. Can be repeated on the opposite side for a double-laced effect.

chain stitch

1. End your first stitch by returning it right next to (if not right into) where you began

2. Before pulling the slack all the way through, enter the needle up to catch it

3. Finish the second stitch like you did the first, by returning right next to where you began

4. Continuing to catch the slack of each stitch, and ending each stitch right next to where you began will create a chain. You can end the chain by anchoring down on the other side of the slack.

couch stitch

Making a couch stitch is nothing more than anchoring down one thread with a second. Thread the first to enter the surface and leave it there. Thread a second and anchor the first down with small whip stitches to hold it in place along the line you are following.

satin stitch

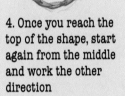

1. Back stitch or split stitch around your shape. Enter again near the middle of the shape at the outer side of the stitch line.

2. Come down on the other side of the shape just to the outer side of the stitch line and at a slight angle

3. Continue to cover the shape by entering on one side and exiting on the other, laying the stitches next to one another

4. Once you reach the top of the shape, start again from the middle and work the other direction

seed stitch

Seed stitch is just a group of small stitches that can vary in density and direction to change the texture of the stitched surface.

French Knot

1. After entering the surface, begin to wrap the slack around the tip of the needle using your finger to hold the thread taut

2. Wrap the thread around the needle a few times, keeping the coil near the base of the stitch

3. Simultaneously pull the coils tight against the needle as you angle the tip of the needle down towards where you began the stitch; exit the surface to make the knot

lazy daisy

1. Begin and end your first stitch at just about the same place

2. Enter the surface to catch the slack of the first stitch

3. After pulling the slack through, anchor the loop down with a small stitch at the outer side of loop

4. Repeat Steps 1-3, and keep their pointed edges toward each other to create a floral design

Bullion Stitch

1. Enter the surface at A, exit at B, then enter at A again

2. Before pulling slack, wrap thread coming out at A around the needle

3. Wrap 5 or 6 times and then hold the coils with one hand as you pull the needle through them with the other

4. Once all the slack is pulled, use the needle to press the coils back neatly, then exit stitch at B to finish

Eyelet Stitch

button hole variation

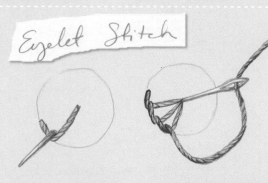

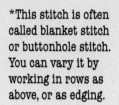

1. Enter on the line of the circle and exit at the center of the circle

2. Before pulling slack, catch it by entering a stitch length away from where you started

3. Continue this way and work around the circle like spokes on a wheel. Anchor the last stitch.

*This stitch is often called blanket stitch or buttonhole stitch. You can vary it by working in rows as above, or as edging.

Coloring Book Collection

Pattern pages 139 and 141

Inspiration

A fabulous source of simple line work for embroidery, particularly when you are making children's items, is a coloring book. I decided to draw my own little objects and characters for this collection but set the stage for play with the charm and simplicity of a storybook in mind. Using the general silhouette shape of each piece, I backed them with printed quilting cotton scraps and then stuffed them with fiberfill. They instantly became a soft toy, perfect for little hands to dream up big adventures. Not to mention that some of the kids kept stealing my drawings for coloring, so the whole process was quite fun for others beside myself.

THREAD:

Anchor six-strand embroidery floss (use six strands)

COLORS:

92, 94, 267, 333, 433, 1035

CLOTH:

Cotton evenweave in mushroom, 20" x 27"

OTHER MATERIALS:

Fiberfill, and scraps of printed quilting cotton.

FINISHED SIZE:

Varies between 3" x 5" and 6" x 8"

Notes

* I used an evenweave for this project simply because I like the texture. I traced all six drawings, using a water-soluble fabric pen and my light table, onto a single piece of evenweave (20" x 27"), leaving plenty of space between each vignette. I also kept each drawing far enough from the fabric's edge so that I could use an embroidery hoop easily.

* Using all six strands of the embroidery floss kept the project running along because I didn't have to stop to separate threads, and it provided a nice thick outline for the drawings. I chose a back stitch for its simplicity (and, of course, French knots for eyes) which earned me some help from Isabela on the stitching.

* After finishing the stitching:

1 I drew a line around the perimeter of each stitched design on the wrong side, simplifying the silhouette a bit and keeping the line about an inch or so away from the work. An important aspect of these line perimeters is to keep them straight along the bottom edge of the drawing. This will help your little one to stand or lean the figure right side up when they are playing, as well as give you a straight edge to blind-stitch closed after stuffing the toy.

2 Once all the silhouette lines were drawn around my stitching, I cut them out of the material, well away from the drawn lines, mostly in square or rectangular shapes. Then I layered them right sides together with a printed fabric of the same general shape and size. I used the drawn lines on the embroidery's wrong side as my machine sewing guide and left an opening along the straightest edge for stuffing. Using a small stitch length is recommended for this and any project that has curves.

3 I then trimmed away, clipped, and notched the seam allowance to keep the curves smooth, turned the piece right side out, smoothed the seams with my fingers from the inside, and stuffed it with fiberfill before blind-sewing the opening closed by hand.

Voilà

From the moment I drew these designs onto cloth my little Roman referred to each one using his own name: *"Is that Roman's birdie?"; "Are you sewing Roman's car, mommy?"* He knew instantly that these sweet and simple toys would be his, and began developing his own little narratives with them before I was even finished. All that is to say, of course, that these make a wonderful set of toys for a little person, and you can easily take custom orders from a three-year-old. Also, what fun these would be enlarged to the size of a bed pillow! Trading out your embroidery needle and floss for a crewel needle and tapestry yarn would make quicker work of completing the stitching at that scale.

Daylight Fading

Daylight Fading

Pattern page 143

Inspiration

I made this blouse for Juliana's friend Sierra, who has such an ethereal yet rich beauty, so I wanted to make something for her that was inspired by the subtle glow at dusk. I kept the hues for the fabric mostly monochromatic but with subtle shade changes in pieces of the construction. The design of the embroidery is not unlike something you might find in a colorful ethnic-inspired blouse. I chose most of the floss colors however, to just barely speak out against the gray background, and only a few that added pops of color and gave the floral design some dimension. The finished work seems as though the floral is emerging from the material itself rather than having been stitched on top of it.

THREAD:
Anchor six-strand embroidery floss (various strands)

COLORS:
189, 232, 235, 280, 281, 334, 400, 401, 850, 872, 921, 1035

CLOTH:
Solid quilting cotton

OTHER MATERIALS:
Sewing pattern and notions for constructing the garment of your choice.

FINISHED SIZE:
Approximately 8" x 8"

PATTERN:
Use the Daylight Fading pattern and your desired sewing pattern (I used my own Painted Portrait Blouse pattern)

Notes

* As suggested in the opening of the Free Works section, I drew out the yoke piece of this pattern onto the cloth, keeping seam allowances in mind before I positioned, transferred, and stitched my design.

* Because I was working on a darker cloth, I chose to transfer the embroidery design using a white transfer paper and a ballpoint pen as a stylus. To make sure that I was positioning the design exactly where I wanted it on the yoke, I actually cut the transfer paper in the shape of the yoke.

* The close-up of the stitch work points out the various stitch styles used in the embroidery. I used various numbers of strands for each style of stitch, so just trust your instincts. I also used a hoop size large enough to encompass the whole work so that I wouldn't have to keep shifting it.

* Once the stitching was complete, I gently prewashed it by hand along with the other materials for the blouse before pressing and constructing the blouse. I didn't interface the back of the stitch work because my sewing pattern calls for lining the yoke.

Voilà

Once the blouse was complete, I couldn't help but add a little stitch detail along the edge of the cuffs and hem where I used a simple blanket stitch (shown on page 85) to echo the subtle shades in the yoke embroidery. I really enjoyed working in these subtle shades, and it has sparked my interest to work more with solid colors and monochromatic stitch work, including single color work. The texture and interest that is created by the stitching alone without a great amount of color is sublime.

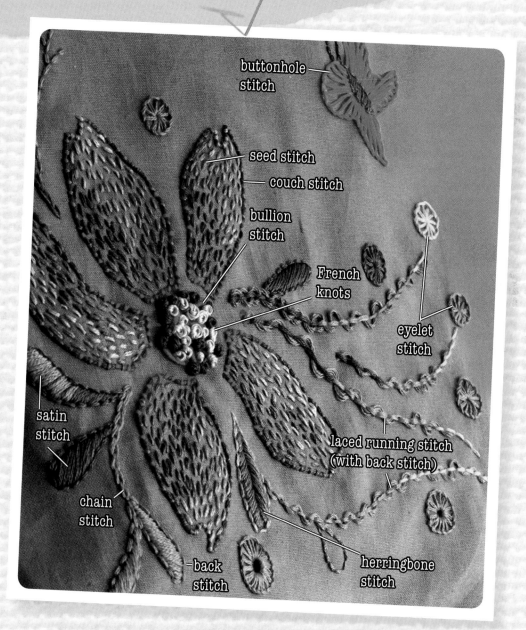

Brace Yourself

Brace Yourself

Inspiration

As much as I love bold and illustrative jewelry, I don't really love wearing bracelets on a regular basis, particularly the metal or heavy kind that can snag clothing (or poke toddlers that I'm holding). But I can always manage to wear friendship bracelets that any of the children have made for me or fabric cuffs that I've made myself because they are so lightweight and comfortable. After I made some charming little ribbon bracelets, I decided it would be nice to add a little more interest and texture to my collection by embroidering some as well. They provide (almost) instant gratification as well as a lovely way to turn some sample embroidery into a finished piece as you practice new stitch styles.

THREAD:
Anchor six-strand floss

COLORS:
203, 228, 238/86, 94/170/279

CLOTH:
Even linen ribbon

OTHER MATERIALS:
Jewelry components, beads, beading needle and thread, lightweight fusible interfacing, Stiffy Fabric Stiffener, and paint brush.

FINISHED SIZE:
Variable

Notes

* To create a bracelet that acts like a bangle, I measured my wrist circumference and added 1½" to it. I marked that length on the evenweave linen ribbon, but left an inch or two at each end.

* For the stitching, I simply treated each bracelet sort of like a stitch sampler. For instance, the citrus-colored one is nothing more than rows of chain stitches, the green one is nothing more than French knots, the blue one is an eyelet stitch (with holes cut out in the center of each circle first so that the eyelets would have a larger "eye"), and the magenta one is a meandering couch stitch.

* After the stitching was complete, I pressed some lightweight interfacing on the wrong side of the bracelet. (Be sure to do this pressing from the wrong side, with the right side of the stitching settled into a plush towel.)

* I sewed the ribbon right sides together, matching up the marks that denoted my measured wrist + 1½". I pressed the seam allowance open and covered its raw edges with another piece of interfacing. The evenweave ribbon is so nice and firm to begin with, but to make it even more like a bangle, I brushed a thick coat of fabric stiffener onto the inner side of the bracelet and let it dry standing up. I also made sure it was shaped into a nice circle as it dried.

Including little beads and jewelry findings into your stitching is a lovely addition and keeps these pieces looking even more like jewelry. The fabric stiffener is lightweight enough that I could still sew beads into place after it was dried.

Voilà

My time creating these bracelets inspired a whole collection of various jewelry projects that included not only embroidery, but also crochet, cross stitch, and many beautiful jewelry components that are designed to frame and feature gorgeous little vignettes of stitching. I've shared a spread of jewelry works in progress with some notes.

Juliana cross stitched a skull & crossbones on scraps of black Aida cloth before mounting them inside these earring frames.

Eleni used my pre-printed cross-stitch fabrics to stitch out one flower to include in a pendant for a necklace.

* A tiny butterfly that I am stitching out on linen ribbon using a simple tent stitch. It's the perfect size for this pendant frame.

* This necklace includes some repurposed pieces of a broken necklace, a crochet strip whip-stitched between two chains, ribbon, and some patches of embroidery.

* There is also a smattering of ribbon scrap, floss, and yarn here and there.

* This bracelet is just two layers of ribbon joined by a blanket stitch on the edges, where I also included some gold: a gold bead in every other stitch.

* With this ribbon bracelet, I made some miniature crochet details all around the perimeter using the blanket stitches on the edges as a base.

Tracing Blossoms

Tracing Blossoms

Inspiration

Taking a cue from pre-printed canvases in needlepoint, I have long enjoyed embroidering onto printed cotton where I often allow the print to guide my direction, color, and even style of work. While it would be perfectly fine to also ignore what is happening in the fabric print (see my Wild at Heart project, page 110) and just go on about my business of stitching whatever I like, for this project I paid careful attention. I chose the fabric (the Coreopsis print from my own Loulouthi collection) for its tonal characteristics, knowing that it would be pretty simple to achieve a striking embellishment with complementary colors of floss by simply following the print. I also like how just stitching over one or two floral vignettes gave me just the scale I had in mind for the design element on the front of sweet Lily's dress.

THREAD:
Anchor six-strand embroidery floss

COLORS:
255, 433, 1092

CLOTH:
Printed quilting cotton

OTHER MATERIALS:
Sewing pattern and notions to complete the baby dress, or a readymade garment.

FINISHED SIZE:
Variable

Notes

* There is no transfer necessary with this project so getting to the fun part was as simple as gathering my fabric, needle, floss, snips, and hoop.
  As recommended previously, I first traced the sewing pattern of the dress onto the cloth before I worked the stitching onto the print.

* I filled all of the leaf, stem, and petal areas with a split stitch, but rather than forming a line with them, I used it more as a fill stitch in order to completely fill sections without any fabric showing through. I also added some French knots and seed stitches as the print dictated.

* Once the design was complete, I backed it with some lightweight, woven fusible interfacing to be sure that Lily wouldn't get any itchies coming from the stitch work and to protect the stitching from wear.

* Another simple example of using a favorite fabric print as the foundation for creating a gorgeous embroidery work is shown on the left. In this instance I let the fabric guide all of my color choices as I made one French knot after another to eventually fill the whole piece.

* If a favorite scrap of cloth is too small to fit into an embroidery hoop, just baste a muslin border around the piece as you work in order to give yourself plenty of room for stitching. You can remove the border later depending on how you might incorporate the work into a sewn item, or simply have it framed.

Voilà

I never tire of this combination of printed fabric and handwork. This must be why I love hand quilting so much. The dialog between the stitches and the prints is so interesting and holds my imagination as I work. The Tracing Blossoms project is very simple and practically foolproof, not to mention that it is a perfect way to introduce embroidery to your children because it's just like coloring with thread. However, just imagine the elaborate works that could be made with this simple concept, but on a larger scale with more color and stitch varieties. It makes my heart race with happiness.

Loves Me Bouquet

Loves Me Bouquet

Pattern page 145

Inspiration

This was a project that just kept growing. I began by translating one of my own fabric prints into a line drawing, and the plan was to simply stitch a line-style embroidery for it. Well, one thing led to another, and I couldn't help but realize this design more fully with a variety of stitch work in deeper concentrations. Perhaps it was because I had only ever seen it as a full-color print that somehow the simple approach seemed unfinished. Whatever the case, it was time intensive, but is likely one of my single favorite personal accomplishments in embroidery. Did that fact have me leaving it alone? Absolutely not. I also wanted to play around with a patchwork border for this work, but one that would support rather than overpower the stitching. So I carefully selected fine, smaller-scale prints in muted versions of the embroidery colors as well as a few pops of bright and deep tones to echo the accents of the bouquet. I kept the strips in the patchwork really narrow at just a finished ¼", to avoid any single material getting too much attention. Follow along with my notes for more tips on stitching and patching the whole work together.

THREAD:
Anchor six-strand embroidery floss (various strand thicknesses, but mostly three)

COLORS:
50, 75, 78, 89, 99, 109, 110, 161, 167, 187, 240, 255, 259, 266, 279, 348, 400, 1031, 1036

CLOTH:
Solid quilting cotton

OTHER MATERIALS:
Scraps of quilting cotton, or ⅛-yard cuts of 12–15 favorite fabrics.

FINISHED SIZE:
Approximately 16 ½" x 20"

Notes

* Because I wasn't sure exactly what this work would become when I started, I began with a fairly large cloth and transferred my design to it using transfer paper and a stylus. I probably could have seen the pattern lines through the pale-gray material at the light table, but I wanted to experiment with the transfer paper (more thoughts about the transfer paper process are offered on page 76).

* This was a work that I picked up and put down an awful lot before it was finished. And sometimes this had me inadvertently using a color of floss in a specific area that I assumed was the one I had started with, only to find I had accidentally switched colors. It was then that I sort of let go of my control over the colors, and let the coloration become inconsistent here and there. At times it was because I ran out of a color, other times it was just because I felt like seeing what would happen if I used the "wrong" color; but all of the little reasons added up to me loving this piece and the process of it all the more.

* Among my stitch style varieties are: chain stitch, satin stitch, seed stitch, split stitch, back stitch, French knot, and couching stitch. Refer back to pages 82–85 for tutorials on how to complete these stitches and have a look at some of those stitches pointed out in the close-up photo on the right to see where they occur.

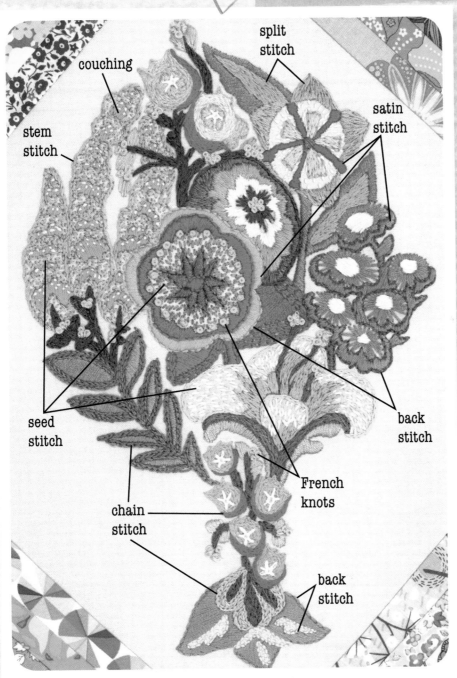

split stitch

couching

stem stitch

satin stitch

seed stitch

back stitch

chain stitch

French knots

back stitch

* Follow these steps to create a strip-piece patchwork around your embroidery once it's complete:

1 Keeping the embroidery at the center of the material, cut the material down to your desired final dimensions plus 1 inch in each direction.

2 Use a paper template that is 9" x 9" to center over the embroidery, turning the square on its point and tracing a perimeter line around on the cloth. (You could also do this with a clear plastic template or a quilt ruler, which makes it easier to see whether you are centering the design.)

3 Cut several strips of printed fabric about 1" x 12" or longer, depending on the size of your piece.

4 Begin laying the printed pieces out along the drawn square perimeter to have a look at them. Continue to add strips to each side all around until you've built out past the edges of the foundation material. I kept rearranging until I liked the color and print balance, and then I took a photo so that I could use it as reference once it was time to sew the pieces. Set aside all pieces.

5 With its right side down, lay a strip of printed material against the foundation piece on the inside of the drawn square, aligning its edge with one drawn side, but making sure that the strip ends are overlapping the two perpendicular drawn lines by an inch or so. Pin in place and sew using a quarter-inch seam allowance along the edge closest to the drawn line. Fold the strip back to reveal its right side (¾" of the strip will be revealed now), and press.

6 Repeat Step 5 with another strip at the next (counterclockwise from the first) side of the square, but be sure to do so over the top of the previously sewn strip, which is facing right side up now. (The next row will be laid down in line with the outer edges of the first strips.) Continue to build out in this manner around each side, going counterclockwise and concentrically until you've filled the foundation fabric with strip piecing.

7 You can now use a straightedge and rotary cutter to trim off excess strips and get your final piece "squared" for the next step. If you'd like to incorporate the finished work into a sewn item, you can begin that now.

8 If you'd like to frame the piece, first sew a border of material a few inches wide around each side of the piece to increase its size and give you some material to wrap around foam core before placing it in a frame. Follow more framing tips on page 122 to finish.

Voilà

I love how the intricacies of the floral stitch work are matched by the intricacies of the florals in the printed fabrics. See how the French knots in the stitching are echoed throughout the fabrics in tiny dots? These similarities between the two elements of design give the piece continuity and some sparkle. I might be interested to see something similar done, but with even thinner strip pieces made from solids that build out in intensity as they reach the edge of the piece. Endless!

Crewel

Crewel work is one of those needlecrafts where my adoration for it far exceeds the number of attempts I have made with it. I imagine I can chalk that up to not really being exposed to it as a young girl. However, if you are like me in that regard, you can take heart if you were exposed to any form of embroidery. But if not, once you've worked your way through a few of the projects in the Embroidery chapter, you'll be ready to approach this gorgeous tradition. There is much overlap in technique between the two disciplines, so the following introduction will focus on those tools and processes that are specific to crewel work.

Common Materials and Tools

As a free style of needlework, incorporating crewel work into items for the home is ideal and welcome. The heavier materials of wool and linen that are traditionally used have somewhat dictated this fact, as has the long and illustrative history of needlecraft. Traditional crewel work is often referred to as *Jacobean Crewelwork*, and was named after the king who ruled the United Kingdom in the seventeenth century (Jacob being the Hebrew form of his name James). His reign saw the height of this stylized form of needlework being stitched onto everything from bed linens to curtains to wall hangings, mostly in wealthier homes.

Today we have every weight, weave, count, style, and color of material available to us, but linen twill survives as the ideal cloth to serve as the foundation for crewel work. It is durable enough to hold the heavier weight of elaborately worked wool threads, and its high thread count offers the perfect base for precise work. That's not to say you shouldn't be encouraged to experiment. I find the combination of a centuries-old process and a modern-day design sensibility quite provocative.

One feature that stands out as unique to crewel work is the use of a wooden slat frame. This frame style requires a somewhat laborious process of attaching your surface material to the four sides by hand-stitching its top and bottom to webbing that is part of the frame, and hand-lacing the sides of the material to the remaining sides of the frame. The construction allows you to continue rolling the top and bottom and to use the side lacework to tighten as you stitch, which is especially important for large and more elaborate works. My description simplifies the process greatly; however, if your intentions for crewel work are sincere and invested, then I highly recommend researching the process, particularly if you will be using the traditional linen twill for your work. It will require a longer list of materials than suggested here, but you'll be left with a secure and durable surface on which to prick and pounce your design (described on page 76). Not to mention that you can take pride in participating in this needlecraft in its most traditional form.

For the sake of my own experimentation with crewel work, I chose to work the Garden Geometry project on page 118 using somewhat traditional processes and materials. I did, however, modify the framing process to suit a roller frame that I already own. For all other work, I used a variety of hoops that were on hand because they suited my chosen materials. It's nice to have a deeper-than-standard hoop for crewel, and you might wrap twill tape or bias strips around the inner or outer rings (or both) to minimize creasing of your material. Additionally, you should take the hoop off any time you put down your work.

I exclusively used Appleton crewel wool for my projects because it seems to be the only single brand available in the U.S. that offers such an expansive palette of colors. It is a two-ply worsted yarn, and like all yarns is dyed in batches, so there could be some small discrepancies between two skeins of the same color purchased at different times or locations. Though you do not separate the plies to use them, you can use any number of strands at once—even a few colors—in your work for various results and textures.

The perfect needle to use for crewel work is called a *crewel needle,* which is narrow and sharp but has an eye large enough to thread wool. A chenille needle is ideal for heavier work because the larger shaft prepares the fabric surface to accommodate the thickness of several strands of wool as you stitch. If you happen to be working stitches that weave through surface work more than they stitch through the material, switch to a tapestry needle so that the blunt tip helps you avoid pricking the yarns and the surface of the material. It's also not a bad idea to have a pair of tweezers on hand to pick out any clipped stitches you are trying to remove.

Stitch Know-how

To pull the loose end from your skein of wool, be sure to choose the end that is toward the inner side of the skein. Pulling on the outer loose end will quickly tangle

your skein, so begin slowly to be sure you have the right end. Thread the wool strand(s) into your needle in a similar fashion to threading tapestry wool, as described on page 53. The recommended cut length of about 15"–18" is the same as for tapestry wool to avoid the yarn becoming threadbare. Crewel often covers the material underneath so densely that you might try beginning each thread with a holding stitch. This is nothing more than a knot at the end of your strand that you "sit" on the right-side surface of your work. To create holding stitches, enter from the right side of the work and be sure to set this knot within an area that will be completely covered; it should be near where you are beginning your work. Bring the needle up and down again to make a tiny stitch into the material about ¼" away from the knot, then another between the first stitch and the knot. You can then tug the knotted end upward to clip right underneath the knot at the base just above the material; the tail should then settle itself into the thickness of the material. Your subsequent stitching will cover the holding stitches, and you can finish threads in a similar manner or by weaving through existing work on the back side.

Stitch Tutorials

If you've practiced some of the stitches shared in the Embroidery chapter, the good news is that there is no need to start over and learn new stitches as all of them will suit crewel work beautifully. However, I've included some additional stitch tutorials here that either exemplify the beautiful transitional shading techniques so commonly found in crewel work, or that really let the wool yarns do their magic.

coral stitch

1. After entering the surface, hold the slack to one side, and exit just behind the slack

2. Before pulling the slack through, enter the surface again just in front of the slack

3. Pull the slack from underneath the surface and hold, before pulling the needle all the way up to finish the knot

4. Continue this process in a line to create a knotted length

long and short stitches

1. Enter the surface near the top of the shape and exit at the very top edge

2. Repeat Step 1, but vary the distance of your starting point from the top edge

3. Begin a second row of stitches that nestle between the previous stitches and vary in length

*This is an excellent stitch for shading by changing color gradually with each new row.

Padded Satin Stitch

1. Shape a row of stitches side by side within your shape, but filling a smaller space

2. Repeat Step 1 over the top of the first fill stitches, going in a perpendicular direction and making a slightly larger shape

* Let the consecutive row grow in size and alternate direction. Follow this process with the satin stitch (page 84) to create a dimensional buildup of thread on the surface.

Herringbone Stitch

1. Begin on one side of the shape and exit on the other side at an upward angle

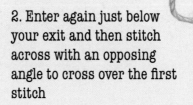

2. Enter again just below your exit and then stitch across with an opposing angle to cross over the first stitch

3. Repeat Step 1, just above where you began the first stitch

4. Continuing to alternate sides and laying each side's stitches right next to each other will create the herringbone design. It is shown here just partially finshed

* This is an excellent stitch for making leaves.

2. Repeat Step 1 by overlapping the first group of stitches with a second group of stitches that lay at a perpendicular angle

1. Cover your shape with long, parallel stitches (straight or angled) from one side to the other, with equal space between them

3. Couch (page 83) the long stitches down at their intersections with smaller stitches

* Varying the densities of the long stitches and the color of the small stitches can create lovely effects.

Wild at Heart

Wild at Heart

Pattern page 147

Inspiration

Working something as monochromatic as leopard spots seemed a lovely opportunity to practice my long and short stitch. Using only two or three colors of wool really helped me practice my technique and not fuss too much with a lot of color changes. As shared in the Tracing Blooms project, I really enjoy applying handwork onto a printed fabric surface, but in this instance I ignored the vintage floral pattern and, rather, worked my own design right over it. The appearance of the provocative leopard spots against the demure floral is a lovely nod to the transition of fashion influences in the late '50s and early '60s.

THREAD:

Appleton crewel wool

COLORS:

303

CLOTH:

Vintage calico cotton

FINISHED SIZE:

Variable

Notes

* I started the long and short stitch at the center of each spot, and worked outward. I also left uneven edges to the spots to emulate the natural leopard fur and to give the design a sketched quality.

* Inspired by my Spotted in the Crowd fabric, this design is really more of a continuous repeat than it is a singular motif, so you could certainly keep repeating and stitching for as long as you like. In that way, this project is more like building and reinventing cloth than it is completing an artwork with handwork.

* Should you decide to include your stitched spots in a garment, be sure to define your seam lines early on (by tracing them onto the fabric first), so that you can keep any stitched areas clear of cut lines. You can always go back into a constructed garment, and add a few spots here and there to join the repeat of the spots smoothly between pattern pieces.

Voilà

I am still debating whether to frame this work or to continue stitching more of it and wear it. If I happen to reel in my enthusiasm for this somewhat and don't make yards of stitched cloth, even a small panel would be gorgeous to include in a dress or a blouse (not to mention a pillow or a bag).

Letters Home

Letters Home

Pattern pages 149 and 151

Inspiration

The plan for this project, like so many, wasn't fully realized for several weeks. I frequently have ideas for two or three separate projects that eventually join themselves into one. For instance, with this project I had planned to embroider an oversized, handwritten cursive word. It wasn't until I had frosted my Eleni's name in cursive onto her birthday cake using several shades of sugary icing that I decided my stitched cursive word should also transition through the whole spectrum. Not until I had been traveling for 10 days away from my family did I decide what the word itself should be. For my free time I had packed linen, a spectrum of wool, a needle, snips, a water-soluble pen, and stationery to write home. Home. At the time I couldn't think of a more beautiful word. I also couldn't think of a better place to rest my head, so I was inspired to make a pillow. For a final touch of comfort, I hand-quilted the background in rows to emulate our favorite quilts as well as the lines of a handwritten letter.

THREAD:
Appleton crewel wool

COLORS:
In color order: 159, 486, 435, 255, 253, 311, 313, 475, 557, 443, 995, 945, 942, 801, 711, 452

CLOTH:
Linen evenweave in natural

OTHER MATERIALS:
Bamboo quilt batting, muslin, fabric for pillow backing—each in pillow dimensions, safety pins, water-soluble marker, straightedge, and zipper (optional).

FINISHED SIZE:
18½" x 24"

Notes

* Feel free to stitch your own handwritten word. For me, developing the cursive pattern was as simple as writing the word in my regular script over and over until I saw one that I liked. I scanned, enlarged, and traced the art with tracing paper a few times to thicken and perfect the lines on paper. Once I was happy with it, I traced the art with a fine black marker and then used a light table and water-soluble pen to transfer to the linen.

* Either follow the color numbers I have listed, or develop your own ever-changing spectrum. Once you've determined your color order, I recommend taping down a cutting of each yarn onto paper in order to keep your place as you stitch. You might even section the traced word with some lines to signal when to switch threads. My stitching is sort of a hybrid between split stitch (page 82) and long and short stitch (page 107). I let the direction of the stitches flow with the direction of the letters.

* Beginning and ending the word with the same darker shade unifies the design. Stitching with that color for a longer expanse than you have with the others in between will anchor the design as well. Notice how I chose to work the color in the areas where the cursive overlaps itself in the "h," "o," and "e." It appears more three-dimensional because

I transitioned the color as though it was a single continuous ever-changing rope that passes in front of and behind making some colors hide and reappear in those overlaps.

* Once the word was completely stitched, I used a water-soluble pen and a clear quilting ruler to mark out straight lines for quilting about every inch.

* After sandwiching a piece of quilt batting between the wrong side of the stitched work and a piece of muslin, I pinned all layers together with curved safety pins to begin the hand-quilting. And yes! I quilted with the wool in a cream color.

* I cut lengths that were a few inches longer than the width of the piece. While this is, of course, longer than what is recommended for a working length of wool, I started the stitching in the center, only pulled my tail through about halfway, and stitched in one direction. Once I reached the end, I knotted on the wrong side, threaded the needle at the other end of the length that was left over, and stitched in the other direction. So even though my cut lengths were about 26" long, I stitched with only half that length at a time.

Voilà

I constructed the pillow just like any other, but included a zipper on the back panel to make removing the cover for dry cleaning easier and to avoid undoing and redoing any blind stitches. I machine-topstitched the pillow all around the perimeter about ½" from the edge for a clean finish.

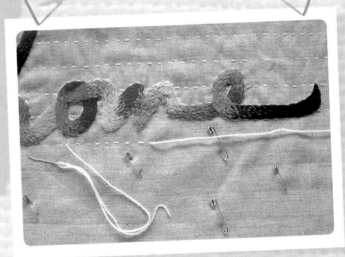

Winter Wool

Winter Wool

Pattern page 153

Inspiration

Since I have made a garment or accessory using a technique from every other discipline in this book, I thought that I should work crewel into something fashion oriented as well. The selection process began in my closet and I naturally gravitated toward using a fall or winter item because of the wool I would be using to stitch the design. I was compelled to use one of my favorite plaid wool skirts because it was a more unexpected choice than a solid, and the neutral tones lend themselves to letting a floral design visually pop off the surface. After all, I had already embroidered or cross stitched onto solids, stripes, florals, and calicos—so it was time for plaid. Getting more interested in the gorgeous shading techniques used in traditional crewel, I decided to design a single flower stem that would incorporate some of them. I chose mostly blue and green wools for the design as they are complements to the red and orange undertones of the neutral plaid. A pop of bright orange relates the design back to the main color family of the skirt material, but in an unexpected way.

THREAD:
Appleton crewel wool

COLORS:
153, 157, 251, 253, 255, 313, 324, 443, 482, 562

CLOTH:
Readymade wool skirt

OTHER MATERIALS:
Tear-away fusible interfacing.

FINISHED SIZE:
Variable

Notes

I used the following process to transfer my design to the skirt:

* After drawing and refining my design, the first decision was where and how to transfer the design to my skirt. Because I was working with a garment that was already constructed, keeping the design towards the lower edge of the skirt made it easier for me to get to it and use an embroidery hoop.

* I used my sewing machine to "trace" this project onto the skirt! I first used a pencil to trace the design from my drawing to a stitch-n-tear type of fusible interfacing that is designed to tear away after stitching. The interfacing is sheer enough to see through for tracing, and I traced the design onto the non-fusible side of the interfacing. Then I fused the interfacing to my desired position on the skirt. I dropped the feed dogs on my sewing machine (many machines have this capability) so that I could use free-motion stitching to trace the drawn lines with stitching. Before stitching onto the skirt, I did practice on a scrap of fabric to refresh my free-motion skills.

* After I was finished, I carefully tore away the interfacing, and used the stitch lines as my guide for crewel work. The machine stitches are easily covered by the thickness of the wool threads, so it's doubtful that any of them will need to be clipped out.

Follow the notes on the close-up of the design for cues on the stitch styles that I used.

Voilà

Now that I've made this happen, no garment in my wardrobe is safe! I think what is particularly nice about this reinvented skirt is that it already had a beautiful drape and interesting design. Carefully selecting the angle at which the flower would fall into an already lovely silhouette is really what makes it work and seem like it was there all along. So with that in mind, have a good look at the garment you'll be embellishing to think about where a wildflower might naturally grow.

Garden Geometry

Garden Geometry

Pattern pages 155
and 157

Inspiration

This is by far the most straightforward approach I have made toward the traditional way of creating a crewel design. This very craft, with its illustrative stitch styles, inspired this row of flowers, which also have simple geometry as their starting point. In fact, I had almost as much fun drawing and coloring the design plan as I did working out the stitches. If any design in this book lends itself to being enlarged and worked across a bigger surface, I would say it's this one. An increased amount of space would give you more opportunity to explore various stitch styles and textures for a field of flowers to get lost in, so modify as inspired!

THREAD:
Appleton crewel wool

COLORS:
101, 106, 207, 253, 421, 424, 452, 505, 522, 524, 557, 801, 891, 942, 944

CLOTH:
Jacobean Linen Twill

OTHER MATERIALS:
Tracing paper, pencil, needle for pricking design; muslin, crushed chalk, and rubber band for creating a pounce pad; wooden rolling frame, string, and large needle for framing work surface; fine pencil for drawing final design; and baby brush for cleaning off excess chalk.

FINISHED SIZE:
8" x 16"

PATTERN:
The design has been tiled onto two pages, so be sure to connect the design before tracing.

Notes

* After making quite an investment on the fine linen twill, I modified the traditional slat-frame construction to suit a less expensive rolling wooden frame that I had on hand for cross stitch and needlepoint. The rolling frame only tightens from the top and bottom, so I added material to the sides of the linen twill to have a border to string some lacing through and tighten the work from the sides.

* I transferred the design using a homemade set of prick and pounce tools (the process of which is described on page 76).

* I crushed some medium-toned colors of school chalk and poured them into a swatch of muslin, which I wrapped shut with a rubber band.

* I used standard tracing paper to trace the design with a pencil, and then laid the drawing over a pillow in order to prick little holes along the drawn lines using an embroidery needle.

* I then pinned the pricked drawing onto the stretched linen and took it outside to "pounce" the chalk pad against the line work, which forced the chalk through the holes and onto the linen twill. After I peeked to be sure that the design was transferred, I carefully lifted off the tracing paper and discarded it.

* Instead of using the more traditional method of painting to connect the lines, I used a fine pencil to draw them. Once that was complete, I flicked the fabric from the back and used a clean baby brush to remove excess chalk dust.

* Follow the stitch style notes on the close-up images for tips on how I combined various stitches.

Voilà

I sort of just enjoy staring at the finished work! I imagine it will get framed in some way, as I feel a little guarded about letting it become a pillow or some such everyday item in this very rough and tumble house of ours. In fact, I even find the laced framing style as a remnant of the working process quite charming. For now, I think I'll just continue to enjoy it as is. My design studio could do with a reminder of the beauty of process.

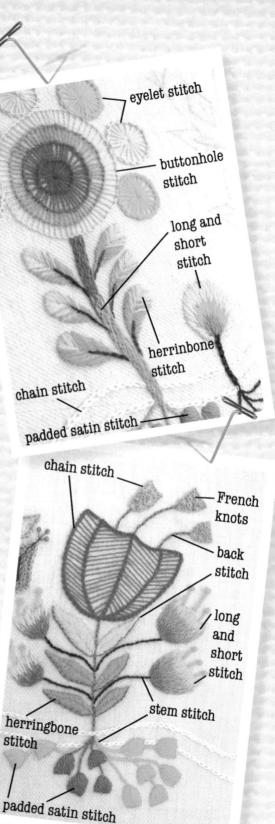

eyelet stitch

buttonhole stitch

long and short stitch

herrinbone stitch

chain stitch

padded satin stitch

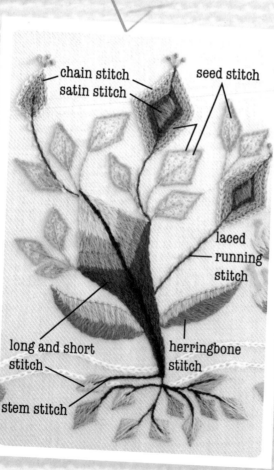

chain stitch
satin stitch

seed stitch

laced running stitch

long and short stitch

herringbone stitch

stem stitch

chain stitch

French knots

back stitch

long and short stitch

stem stitch

herringbone stitch

padded satin stitch

Finishing

This section is devoted to tying up any loose ends, so to speak, as you consider how to finish and care for your stitched work for years to come. It's a great idea to read through these notes before beginning any of the projects to help you understand the possible uses and requirements for your works.

Washing

Before you've even finished stitching any of the works in this book, it's wise to keep the care of their materials in mind as you determine how your piece will be used. Some purchased materials are better than others at expressing the recommended care of the fibers on their packaging, but it's worth it to do your homework and find out. Always use only colorfast threads for your work, because you are so often stitching them onto a light-colored background where bleeding will show up easily. Do not prewash Aida cloth or needlepoint canvas before stitching as you will remove some of the sizing that helps to keep the material stiff, which allows you to avoid using a frame if you so choose.

Of all of the materials that I've worked with in these projects, I only prewashed in two cases: the crewel linen twill before I stitched the Garden Geometry project (page 118), and the materials for the Daylight Fading project (page 89) after I stitched it but before I constructed the blouse. When deciding whether to use dry clean–only or hand-wash materials, keep in mind how you will use each item once it's finished. For those items that will (hopefully) never be washed but kept in a frame, it's a good idea to take some protective steps in their framing to avoid them being stained. When you wash any of the stitched works, I recommend following any available instructions for the materials, but generally you should wash in cold water by hand, with a mild detergent, and hang or press to dry.

Pressing

Make sure your iron is clean and free of residue before you begin. When you need to press a piece, which is often after stitching and before framing or sewing it into another project, take the fiber content into consideration. Cotton floss and threads used in cross stitch and embroidery will perform just fine under a steam iron, and your main concern is taking care not to crush or flatten the texture of your work. Lay a clean, plush towel on your ironing board and settle the stitched piece right side down onto the towel before steam pressing from the back. This allows the uneven surface of your stitching to settle into the fibers of the towel and stay plump. I sometimes remove the towel to press out the surrounding unstitched material if necessary. I also use a spray bottle of water to mist over the whole piece if some stubborn wrinkles require it.

In general, you should avoid ever pressing a needlepoint work. Needlepoint often requires a blocking step (described shortly) that will, for the most part, eliminate the need to press the piece. Should you need to press a crewel work piece, avoid the iron touching the wool yarns. You can try placing muslin between the iron and the wool and steam pressing lightly from the back, and then following the same towel instructions as in the previous paragraph. Do just a little at a time at first and check your results. Additionally, you may try simply steaming the piece with the iron without actually touching the piece to freshen it up. In all instances of pressing, tread lightly at first to make sure your heat settings are appropriate before continuing with the whole piece.

A needlepoint canvas, much like a crocheted or knitted work, needs to be blocked after it's been completed and before it is included in a sewn item or framed because the stitching process can warp the canvas out of shape a bit. There are some rare cases where you can avoid blocking either because the piece might be small enough and not at all warped, or because the piece is created with less traditional materials and with a stitch that does not bias the cloth, as with my Star-Crossed Love project (page 65).

In all other instances, the process of blocking actually begins before you've made even one stitch. The first step is to take a good measurement of your working area on the canvas and make note of it. This is the dimension that your piece will need to be blocked (stretched) to once it is complete. The process of blocking is not difficult but a little time consuming, and if you've done this with other projects, then you already know the general steps. The following is a brief description of the process. Keep in mind that there are professional services that will do this for you.

1   Using a blocking board that you've purchased (or a homemade version made from wood and covered in material marked with the dimension lines of your piece on it), find and mark the four corners within the grid provided to note the dimensions of your piece.

2   Remove any thread swatches or masking tape attached to the canvas. If your wool is washable, you can immerse it in cold water before folding a dry towel around the front and back of it and rolling it up to press out excess water. Or you can dampen the piece using a spray bottle to saturate but not soak it.

3   Let the piece rest for a few minutes after it's been dampened; then stretch it continually with your hands for a bit, taking turns between opposing sides to start preparing it to be blocked.

4   If the piece uses simple tent stitch, you can rest it right side down; if it is a decorative stitch with more texture, you should rest it right side up on the blocking board. Match the corners of the worked area of the canvas to the corner markings on the blocking board, and pin the canvas in place right next to the stitching using T-pins (or safety pins) at an angle that points the top of the pin away from the work. (If you're using a wooden board, use a staple gun instead.)

5   Continue to pin several more pins along each side of the piece, stretching it onto its dimension lines, and keeping your pins about ½" apart. This will probably require a little muscle, so ask for help if you need an extra set of hands.

6   Once the piece is all pinned into place, it will likely take up to a day or two until it's completely dry, so be patient. Some badly warped pieces might take a second or even third blocking session to correct, which will become apparent after the piece has been removed and rested for awhile. However, a repeat blocking will be much easier than the first.

NOTE: There are some methods for blocking that require some an additional stiffening paste to be applied to the back of the work after it has dried but before it has been removed from the blocking board. This is recommended only if you are framing the piece.

Framing

You can, of course, hire a professional framer and if you do so, be sure they have experience in working with your specific type of project. But if you'd like to try it yourself, keep in mind that for framing any of the works in this book, there are two general methods: those for needlepoint and those for all other works. The other works such as cross stitch, embroidery, and crewel work are similar because their base cloths, while woven differently, can be framed and handled in a common way. I'll first go through some steps for framing this larger group of works and then point out some variations on the process for framing needlepoint canvas.

To frame your piece, you need a frame; acid-free foam core; quilt batting (optional); small, flat head straight pins; needle and thread; backing board (cardboard); tape; butcher paper; and glue. Follow these tips for framing:

1   Determine how much of the unworked cloth around the stitching you would like to have showing, but make sure that the frame's opening size is smaller than the total size of your cloth by a few inches in each direction. Select your frame size and either have it custom made or purchase a readymade frame.

2 Cut a piece of foam core and backing board in the same dimensions as the back opening of your frame (this will be larger than the open window from the front of the frame, due to the lip making the frame opening smaller from the front). You can also cut a piece of thin quilt batting to the same size of the foam core and layer the batting over it.

3 Lay your clean, pressed work over the foam core with the right side facing up, and center the design within the foam core board. Regardless of whether you've layered quilt batting underneath, it might also become necessary to place another layer of material right underneath the piece in order to avoid seeing any contrasting color of board or batting peeking out between the weave of something like black Aida cloth.

4 Use just one small, straight pin in the center of the foam core on each side, and then two at both sides of each corner to keep the work in place. Don't press the pins all the way into the board yet, but pick up the board so the fabric perimeter can fall away as you check to be sure you are happy with the positioning.

5 Once you are happy with the positioning, push the pins all the way into the board, keeping the angle in line with the foam core so that they don't poke out of the front or back. Continue to place pins between the first few pins about every ½" or so, and smooth the fabric as you go so that it is somewhat taut, but not overly so as you push in each pin. (You can tap them in with a small hammer if it bothers your fingertips.)

6 After you've pinned all around, fold the corner points of the excess material toward the center back of the foam core and temporarily pin it in place, only slightly entering the back surface with the pin. Then fold in the top, bottom, and sides, which creates mitered corners of material at each corner. Pin this in place, too.

7 Whipstitch each pair of angled folds to each other from the inner corner to the outer corner, and knot to finish. Continue this until all corners are sewn. (I like to spray a layer of Scotchguard on the piece because I don't typically use glass over my handworks when framing.)

8 Place the work into the frame, and lay the backing board piece over it. Tape the backing board to the frame back around all the edges. You can add a layer of butcher paper (cut it just slightly smaller than the outer dimensions of the frame) with some glue spread around all the edges.

9 Add any framing rings or wires to the back of the frame through the butcher paper.

The needlepoint variation of framing follows some of the same general steps, but with some exceptions and additions as follows:

- You do not want any of the excess canvas showing around the perimeter of the work. The front open window of the frame should measure about ½" smaller in each direction than your worked needlepoint dimensions. (This causes the frame's lip to cover just ¼" of needlepoint all around.)

- When wrapping the needlepoint canvas around the foam core, use the pins around the perimeter just as a temporary holding solution so that you don't have to add quite as many pins or push them in all the way.

- Fold the top and the bottom around the back of the foam core and toward each other first. Using a hand-sewing needle and a buttonhole twist, anchor and knot the thread into the canvas, starting in the middle of the top a few rows away from the canvas edge. Then pass the needle across and through the center of the bottom canvas edge a few rows away from its edge. Continue back and forth between the top and the bottom, gradually heading toward one side, lacing them together and tightening the canvas onto the foam core as you go. Be sure not to tighten so much that you bend the foam core. Now repeat from the center of the top and bottom and head toward the other side.

- Repeat with the opposing sides of the canvas to finish preparing the piece for framing.

Sewing

Sewing cross stitch, embroidery, or crewel work into a variety of projects really doesn't require anything extraordinary outside of the typical steps of your sewing project. However, I tend to be very conscious of protecting the wrong side of the work when the project will be worn or laundered frequently. If you have the opportunity to fuse some lightweight woven interfacing onto the back of the work, it will serve very well to keep the stitches in place and provide a smooth back surface to the work.

Sewing with a finished needlepoint canvas is not as hard as it may seem. I think it's a good idea to work two or three extra rows of tent stitch around the perimeter of the work. This way, when you machine sew the work to a pillow backing, for example, you can pass your stitching right between the design and the extra rows. This helps avoid any unworked canvas showing and also allows the entire design that you've stitched to show in the final piece. When sewing a pillow, I like to sew a zipper into the pillow back, before sewing it to the needlepoint front, so that I never have to blind-stitch the needlepoint and backing together by hand. You can then pull the pillow through to the right side through a partially opened zipper. You will want to trim off excess canvas a few rows away from the stitched perimeter, but I do not recommend snipping off the seam allowance corners before turning through to the right side. Rather, fold them in over each other neatly at the corners and push them through one at a time. It might feel bulky at first, but after some practice, you will come to appreciate the firm edges and overall body the needlepoint canvas gives a pillow.

top left

outer, upper left

join this edge to B

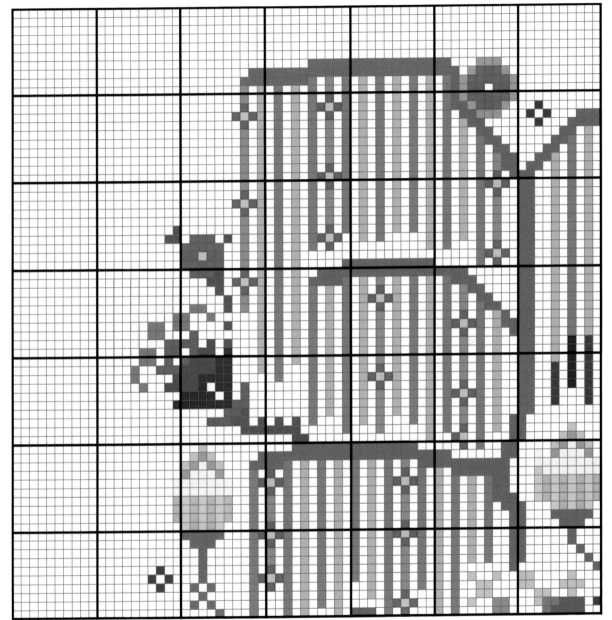

join this edge to C

Menagerie at Midnight A

join this edge to A

outer, upper right

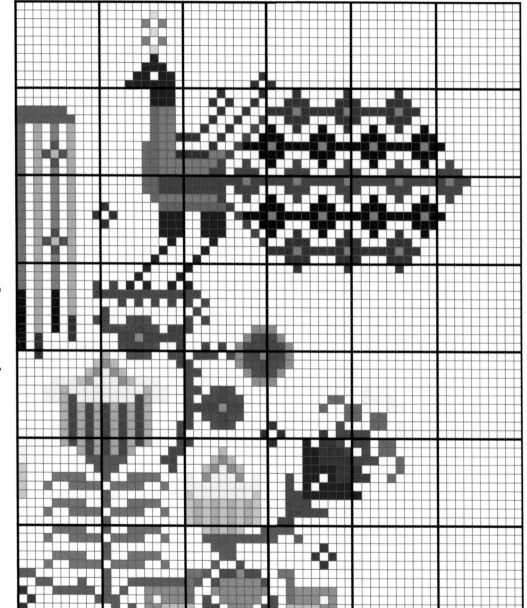

join this edge to D

Menagerie at Midnight B

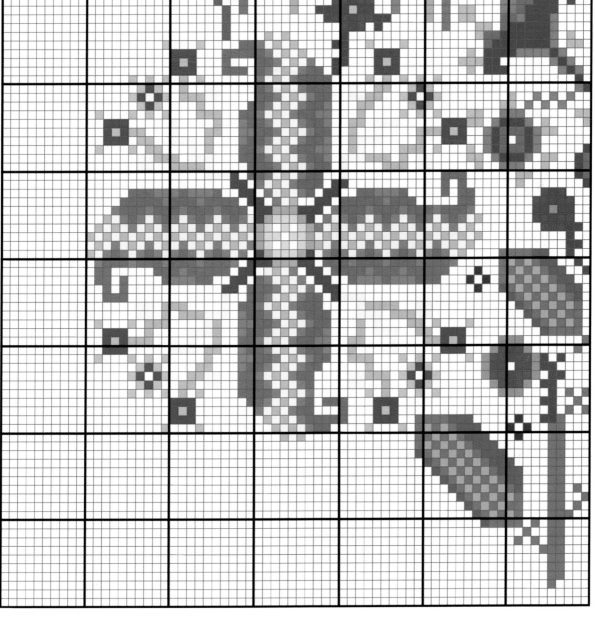

outer, lower left

join this edge to D

bottom left

Menagerie at Midnight C

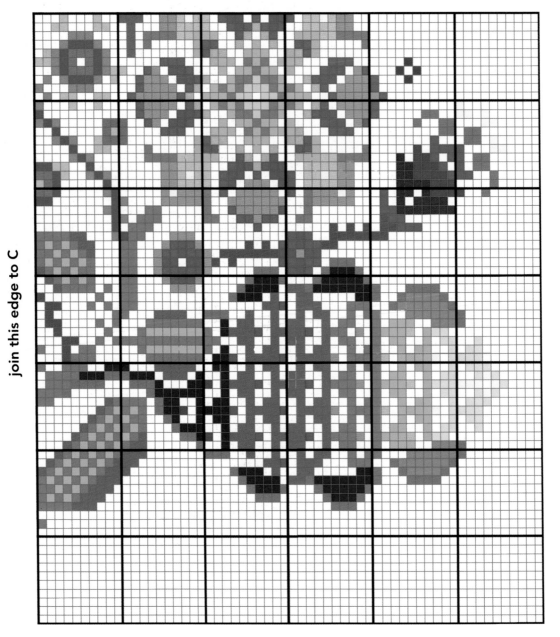

Menagerie at Midnight D

Four Tiles: Spring Sprouting

Four Tiles: Spiritual Center

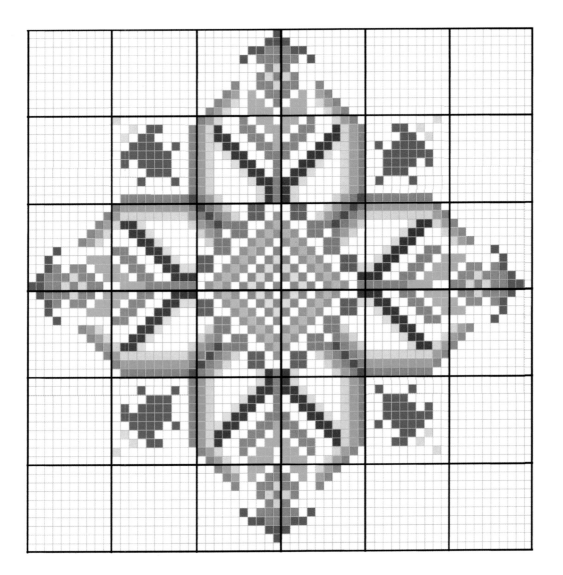

Four Tiles: Terrace Blooms

Four Tiles: Perpetual Motion

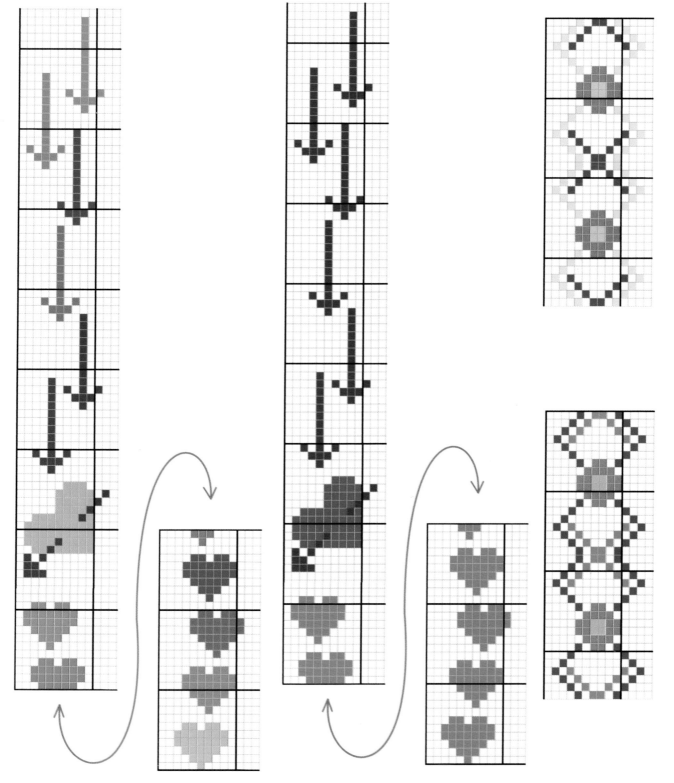

Border Beauties

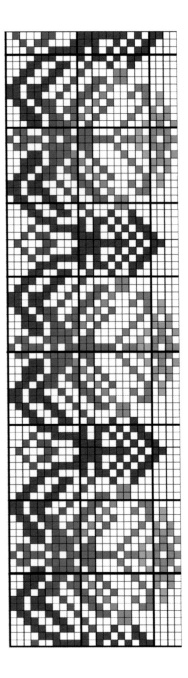
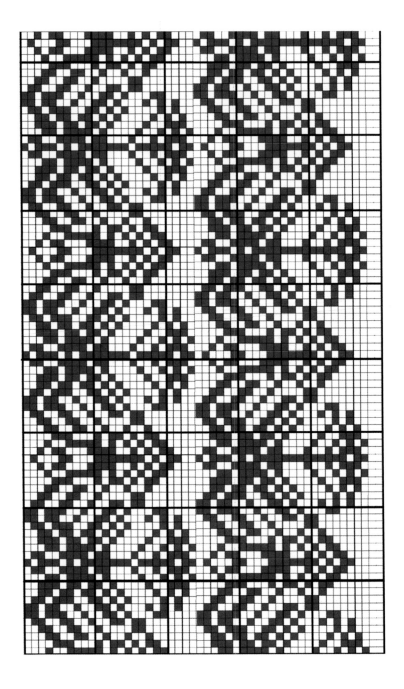

Waves of Plenty

AlphaCute: A through M

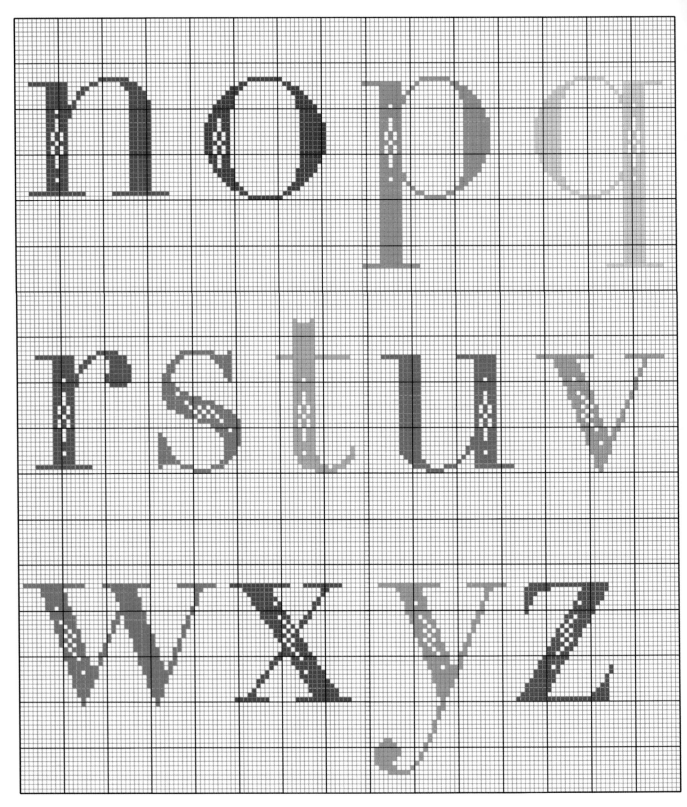

AlphaCute: N through Z

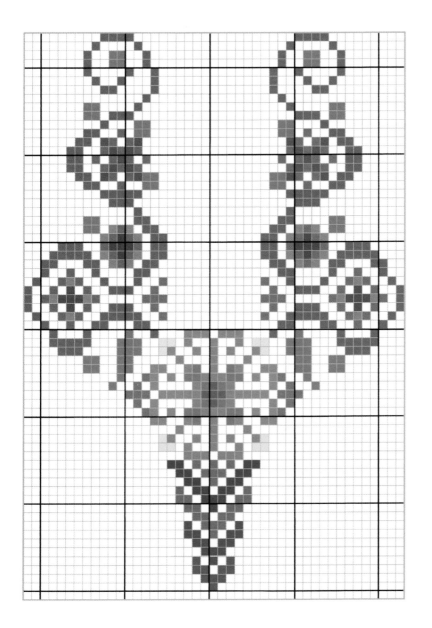

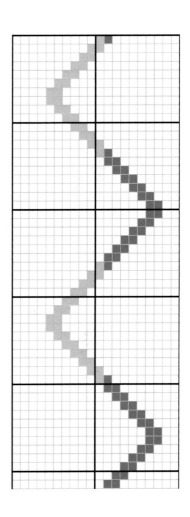

Crossing the Line

Nouveau Needle Cushion

Coloring Book 1

Coloring Book 2

Daylight Fading

Loves Me Bouquet